GREAT HOUSES
OF EUROPE

GREAT HOUSES OF EUROPE

FROM THE ARCHIVES OF COUNTRY LIFE

MARCUS BINNEY

PHOTOGRAPHS BY ALEX STARKEY

AURUM PRESS

From Alex to Veronica, for suffering his long absences.
From Marcus to Anne, for constant help both on and off location.

First published in Great Britain 2003 by Aurum Press Limited
25 Bedford Avenue, London WC1B 3AT

Text copyright © 2003 by Marcus Binney
Photographs copyright © *Country Life* Picture Library

A catalogue record for this book is available from the British Library.

ISBN 1 85410 849 2
10 9 8 7 6 5 4 3 2 1
2007 2006 2005 2004 2003

Design by James Campus
Originated by Colorlito-CST Srl, Milan
Printed and bound in Singapore by CS Graphics

Frontispiece: Trompe l'œil *decoration at Villa Lechi, Brescia, Italy.*
Front endpaper: *The family coat of arms at Palazzo Albrizzi, Venice, Italy.*
Rear endpaper: *The* singeries *ceiling in the Winter Apartment at Schloss Brühl, Cologne, Germany.*

THE COUNTRY LIFE PICTURE LIBRARY

The *Country Life* Picture Library holds a complete set of prints made from its negatives, and a card index to the subjects, usually recording the name of the photographer and the date of the photographs catalogued, together with a separate index of photographers. It also holds a complete set of *Country Life* and various forms of published indices to the magazine. The Library may be visited by appointment, and prints of any negatives it holds can be supplied by post.

For further information, please contact the Librarian, Camilla Costello, at *Country Life*, King's Reach Tower, Stamford Street, London SE1 9LS (*Tel:* 020 7261 6337).

ACKNOWLEDGEMENTS

In writing about the houses in this book, I have consulted many people who have provided valuable insights. These include John Cornforth at *Country Life*, John Harris, the late Hugh Murray Baillie, Robin Middleton, Richard Haslam, Gervase Jackson-Stops and Mary-Anne Stevens. I had the benefit of discussing many of these houses at the Victoria & Albert Museum with Peter Thornton and his colleagues in the Department of Furniture and Woodwork, notably John Hardy, Simon Jervis and the late Clive Wainwright, always ready to impart his fund of knowledge of nineteenth-century decoration and furniture. Brent Elliot gave me many useful leads on historic gardens. Above all, my thanks are due to Alastair Laing, whose encyclopaedic knowledge of European art history and acute eye were repeatedly at my disposal.

In France, my thanks to Edith de Richemont and Vincent Bouvet; in Italy, to Frances Clarke and Peter Lauritzen; in Spain, to Vicente Lléo Cañal; in Sweden, to Ove and Elisabet Hidemark and Arne Losman. Among owners of the houses, my special thanks to the duc de Luynes and the marquis de Contades in France; the late Marchesa d'Amico; to Fernando d'Orey in Portugal; to the Duke and Duchess of Segorbe in Spain. In Germany I received invaluable help from Dr Wilfrid Hansmann at Schloss Brühl, Dr Klaus Merten at Weikersheim, and the late Professor Martin Sperlich at Peacock Island.

Alastair Layzell, producer of the thirty-nine-part series *Mansion: Great Houses of Europe*, provided me with a welcome opportunity to revisit a number of the houses in this book (as well as many others) while filming the programmes.

My wife, Anne, who often travelled with Alex Starkey and me, was an important member of the team. Above all, this book is a tribute to Alex, who as well as taking infinite pains over the photography of every single house, was the best of companions.

The all-important invitation to write this book came from Michael Hall, the deputy editor of *Country Life*; my thanks also to *Country Life*'s editor, Clive Aslet, and the architectural editor, Jeremy Musson. Camilla Costello and Olive Waller in the *Country Life* Picture Library provided invaluable help in making photographs and transparencies available. Trevor Woods made most of the black-and-white prints when the articles were originally published.

At Aurum, my thanks to Clare Howell and Karen Ings and to James Campus, the designer of the book. Finally, I am indebted to Tony Moxhay and John Swift of the Colour Company for their work on the colour images.

LIST OF ARTICLES

The chapters in this book are based on articles that originally appeared in *Country Life*. The articles were all mine, with the following exceptions: Kasteel De Haar by Clive Aslet and Heimerick Tromp; Casa de Pilatos by Gervase Jackson-Stops and Vicente Lléo Cañal; and Palacio de Oca by Gervase Jackson-Stops. All photographs are by Alex Starkey.

CONTENTS

FINDING ever more handsome, well-furnished country houses to fill the weekly issues of *Country Life* has long been a challenge. I joined the magazine in 1968 as architectural writer, shortly after John Cornforth had succeeded Mark Girouard as architectural editor. This was a time of rising taxation, and there was a real fear that it might become steadily more difficult to find suitable houses to write about. A new dimension was added to the relentless quest for houses when the magazine began to use colour photography, initially principally in the *Country Life Annual*, which was published in the autumn each year. The state rooms of Blair, Houghton, Longford, Mereworth and Powys had featured in illustrious succession, but John Cornforth was concerned that it might be hard to find more sequences of grand, colourful interiors ablaze with gold leaf and rich velvet.

The result was that I found myself setting off with Alex Starkey, the magazine's staff photographer, first to France, then to Germany and Italy and later to Austria, Portugal and Sweden. John Cornforth, meanwhile, began to write about houses in Holland and Denmark, followed by Gervase Jackson-Stops and Clive Aslet.

The photographs of all these houses were taken by Alex Starkey, *Country Life*'s last staff photographer, who retired in 1989. Alex and I would set off to Dover in his station wagon, his many photographic cases concealed beneath black cloths, hoping to catch the SS *Chantilly*, which was used by the French for training chefs – the food was infinitely better than on the sister ship, the *Compiègne*. On our first trip to France, in 1970, we were nearly sent back as soon as we arrived, for neither of us knew that to import professional equipment into France we needed a *carnet*, which involved going to the Westminster Chamber of Commerce and paying in a cash sum equivalent to the value of the cameras as a deposit held against their return. Fortunately, a very helpful Calais agent appeared and secured us the necessary documents on the spot, explaining that people going on fashion shoots to the south of France, Rome and other exotic locations had acquired the habit of selling off the clothes when their work was complete and spending a few days living in high style on the proceeds. *Carnets* were supposed to put a stop to this.

Concerned to keep expenses to a minimum, we had set off with a *Les Routiers* guide, good for food but less so, we soon discovered, for places to stay. Alex was a very light sleeper, and after a stay in a hostelry set on a busy crossroads, outside which heavy lorries ground through their gears all night long as they climbed the hill, we turned to the *Michelin* guide, eating well – and usually sleeping soundly – around Europe. By the standards of today's magazine, our trips were long: two or even three weeks at a time, photographing three or four châteaux in one trip, or driving over the Alps into Italy and returning through Germany to villas and *Schlösser*.

The great virtue of going with the photographer was the opportunity to explore and study houses in detail over several days. There was no question of leaving until we had photographed the exterior in sun; this was essential when using black-and-white film, and if this meant staying on for a sixth day, as it did at Meillant, near Bourges,

where we sat under lowering grey clouds, or Oca, in Galicia, where it rained relentlessly in June, we did so. Overcast weather – 'Sod's law,' Alex used to say – also greatly slowed down interior photography, particularly in large, dark rooms with few windows set in thick walls. There were times when Alex would complain, 'I can't even get a reading on the bloody meter.' This would mean exposures of twenty minutes, half an hour or even longer. On one occasion, my wife, Anne, was sent down the grand staircase of Schloss Ellingen to fetch Alex a Kit-Kat with the assurance she wouldn't show in the exposure as she walked down and back up again.

These long exposures were the result of using plate film, initially whole plate (8½ by 6½ inches) for the big shots, and later increasingly a Gandolfi 4 by 5 inch that had been specially made for Alex. For small details, Alex would occasionally use a 35mm camera. Most architectural shots involved a wide-angle lens, with the perspective correction offered by the rising front of a plate camera. To achieve sharp-focus exposures, it was necessary to 'stop down' to the smallest possible lens aperture. Where in reasonable light out of doors an exposure of one-tenth of a second would be appropriate, two minutes might be necessary indoors in good light. Due to sensitivity variations in multi-layer colour film, the speed and colour balance are badly affected by the extremely long exposures needed in dark interiors. In the 1960s and 1970s colour sheet film for tungsten light was rated at 24 ASA and this often necessitated exposures of an hour or so when light levels were very low. A light meter was all but useless under these conditions. Alex would straddle a range of different exposures giving varied times of say fifteen and thirty minutes and even an hour. This in turn created possible problems with vibrations in the floor or occasionally of the film itself 'blipping' within the camera, especially when the atmosphere was hot and humid. Today's films are a great deal faster, meaning that most of these problems have been eliminated. Knowing that he would never have the opportunity to return if things went wrong, Alex would take up to ten exposures and repeat shots if light improved significantly. Several key shots – both inside and out – would almost invariably need to be taken in the middle of the day, leading to agonising pangs of hunger as lunch was delayed to 2.30 or 3 o'clock. The worst case was Bussy-Rabutin in Burgundy, where the custodian only came with a tour on the hour and would not open the doors at any other time. We were locked in the Château from 11.30 till 2 o'clock with no prospect of rushing out to take a picture when the sun was right, let alone of slipping down to the pleasant-looking village for a quick lunch.

When we began, colour pages were still rare in *Country Life*. And even when colour was used, limitations of space meant that full justice could rarely be done to more than a few of Alex's photographs; they would not all achieve the whole-page reproduction that they deserve.

Left: *Villa Torrigiani, near Lucca, with its abundance of statues on the roof balustrades and filling the niches and loggias.*

Schloss Stolzenfels on the Rhine. The pergola in the castle garden frames the view like a stage set.

Alex's greatest skill lay in lighting interiors. Many photographers will say today that they prefer to use natural light as much as possible, but in those days, especially with large-format colour transparencies, this presented formidable problems. Large rooms were often dark, windows and shutters were not easy to open fully, and heavy curtains sometimes stole further light. A big interior shot could take most of a morning to prepare. Alex's trick was to use large sheets of white paper to reflect light into rooms – laid out across the floor and draped over furniture and casement windows. On a few occasions when light was seriously low, Alex would make use of a 2-kilowatt tungsten lamp to reflect light off the windows in imitation of daylight. Otherwise, a minimum of electric light was used, carefully balanced to avoid creating shadows or used to fill in darker areas. In Alex's photographs, you will never see shadows cast by furniture legs (unless by sunlight) – let alone the crossed shadows too often visible under furniture when multiple lights or flash are used.

Above all, the aim was to find houses that retained atmosphere. We were looking for remarkable interiors, rooms with fine panelling and plasterwork and – in Italy – frescoes; for early wallpapers and fabrics, 'grand hangs' of pictures and tapestries. On occasion, the decorative ensembles would extend to the bedrooms as well. The ideal is usually a house that remains in active private ownership, but some of the finest and most complete interiors in this book have been preserved in other ways, particularly in Germany, where, at the end of World War I, the Prussian castles and those of other ruling princes were taken over by the State and are now run by the individual regions or Länder.

The great houses in this book range from the late-medieval Castello di Fenis in the Val d'Aosta to the Villa Kerylos, built on the sea in 1902–07 beside Cap Ferrat as the French Riviera was becoming fashionable. The largest of the houses, Schloss Eggenberg at Graz in eastern Austria, is an archetypal grand Central European residence of a powerful noble family. The smallest is Bagatelle at Abbeville, a *pavillon de plaisance* built for a rich textile manufacturer.

Peacock Island, outside Berlin, though a royal estate, is not a palace but rather a collection of follies including a *Schlosschen*, or Little Schloss, looking like a fantasy in a chinoiserie wallpaper. Schloss Brühl, by contrast, was the summer residence of the Archbishop-Elector of Cologne, built on the grandest scale.

No less interesting is the question of when these houses were used. The Villa Lechi was a June retreat from Brescia that came into use again in the hunting season from September to December. Kasteel de Haar, in Holland, only came to life during one intense month-long country-house party, a tradition that continues to this day. The Margravine Sibylla Augusta of Baden-Baden came to Schloss Favorite in summer; the Hohenlohes went to Weikersheim to hunt the abundant game. The Quinta da Regaleira, like all the villas at Sintra, was an escape from the heat of Lisbon. The Palacio de Oca was very much the centre of a working farm. Casa de Pilatos was an aristocratic town residence, built around arcaded courtyards that provided cool even in hot summer, witness to how the Spanish fell in love with the Moorish way of life after the Reconquista. The two other town houses in this book, the Hôtel de Lauzun in Paris and the Palazzo Albrizzi in Venice, are evidence that the most sumptuous interiors can be found in houses that outside are relatively plain.

Some of the builders of these houses were scions of ancient aristocratic families; others were self-made men whose rise to power had been meteoric, such as Hans Ulrich Fürst von Eggenberg. An interesting group were both soldiers and men of taste. Karl Gustav Wrangel, born at Skokloster in 1613, was to become one of Sweden's greatest commanders, to be compared with Wallenstein in the Empire or Turenne in France. The builder of the Castello di Guarene in Piedmont, Conte Carlo Giacinto Roero, was responsible for the design of a series of fortifications protecting Turin in the War of the Spanish Succession. Louis-Georges-Erasmé, marquis de

Villa Torrigiani. The proscenium arch of the private theatre at the top of the house.

Castello di Fenis, Italy. The sixteenth-century wooden galleries around the sheltered castle courtyard.

Contades, who rebuilt Château de Montgeoffroy on the Loire in 1772–75, was maréchal de France.

It may be fortuitous, but the men and women who built these houses were consistently industrious. The young duc de Chevreuse, who began the Château de Dampierre in the 1660s, may have owed much of his fortune to his young bride, the seventh daughter of Colbert Louis XIV's great minister. But the Duke, Saint-Simon records, had 'an aptitude for work and all forms of science'. Théodore Reinach, who built the Villa Kerylos in 1902–07, was the son of a rich banker but also an immensely energetic scholar and a professor at the Sorbonne. The newly married Reventlows of Schloss Emkendorf had visited Rome in 1783–84 on their grand tour but then came to London, where the young Count had been appointed Danish ambassador to Britain.

Numerous great houses in Europe have lost their contents as a result of wars, revolutions and the abandonment of primogeniture. For *Country Life*, we were looking for houses that were still well furnished, or where decorative schemes were still largely complete. Schloss Brühl may have little furniture, but the *tout ensemble* of dazzling *scagliola*, ravishing plasterwork and astonishing ceiling frescoes makes the interior among the most breathtaking in Europe. Montgeoffroy retains not only Louis XVI furniture and chaste pearl-grey boiseries but also eighteenth-century fabrics in the bedrooms. At Guarene, there are late-eighteenth-century Chinese wallpapers acquired in England. At the Villa Kerylos, every element of furniture and furnishing designed for the house survives in its original place.

Dampierre is a rare example of a grand château that escaped the Revolution intact. When the Duke and his family were arrested in 1794, a handsome daily provision of food and game arrived from the Château, most of which was sequestered by the governor of the gaol, who naturally did not wish to lose so fine a source of supply by precipitately sending his guests to the guillotine.

The twenty-five houses in this book are just a sample of the wealth of great houses in Continental Europe. The interiors and exteriors illustrated here can but serve as a taste of the astonishing creativity among artists, architects, craftsmen and patrons waiting to be explored, enjoyed, chronicled and cared for.

ONE

CASTELLO DI GUARENE

PIEDMONT

Towards 1700, as the great maritime republics of Venice and Genoa edged towards decline,
Piedmont emerged as a vigorous independent state in which the arts flourished as never before. This ascendancy is associated
above all with the reign of Victor Amadeus II (1675–1730), who at last secured the long-contested Alpine borders of his duchy with France
and transformed it into a kingdom by procuring the throne of Sicily – exchanged with some reluctance for the throne of Sardinia
after the Peace of Utrecht in 1720.
This feeling of vigour, confidence and prosperity remains alive to this day, particularly in the rich, fertile country
around Guarene, long famous for its epicurean delights.

The house and village stand a few miles to the north of Alba, the centre of a region that has been called the Perigueux of Italy. The surrounding hills provide quantities of truffles – black, white and marbled – and on their slopes are some of the region's finest vineyards. The Castello di Guarene looks across the valley of the Tanar to Barberesco, which, with Barolo, provides the best wine in Piedmont. From Alba to Guarene the road rises sharply from the plain, climbing through the village past a succession of small Baroque churches, and the house does not reveal itself until you emerge from the narrow streets into the full glare of the sun and the shadeless courtyard immediately in front of it. The massive terrace on which the house is built affords breathtaking views across the valley to other hilltops clustered with villages.

The Castello stands on the site of a medieval castle, which became a fief of the Roero family as early as 1388. By the early eighteenth century, the castle was in ruins and Conte Carlo Giacinto Roero decided to demolish it and replace it with a new house, built to his own designs, to serve as a summer retreat from Turin.

Preceding pages (left): The Castello stands on a massive terrace at the top of the village, surveying the surrounding vineyards. It was begun in 1726 to the designs of its owner, Conte Roero di Guarene.
(right): The clipped yews in the formal garden stand like so many chess pieces, perfectly complementing the clipped hedges of box and beech.

Left: The Galleria, decorated in 1774–76. The furniture, although it looks French in style, is Piedmontese.

Above (left): The Camera Blu, dating from 1760; (right): The Chinese Bedroom, with wallpaper imported from London in 1774.

His other architectural works include the remodelling of the family palace in Turin, designs for the Palazzo Avogadro della Motta in Vercelli and the Bishop's Palace in Cagliari. His interest in architecture had developed during the years he spent in the Piedmontese army between 1698 and 1707. This was a time of acute danger for Piedmont, for at the very moment of the Duke of Marlborough's great victories at Blenheim and Ramillies against Louis XIV, the Duchy was almost overrun by the French. By 1706, Turin itself was under siege and catastrophe was averted only by the arrival of the dashing Prince Eugène of Savoy with fresh troops. During the war, Conte Carlo was responsible for the design of a series of fortifications (his portrait in the Castello shows him with a plan of one of them in his hand).

The foundation stone of the new house was laid on 13 September 1726, and the family was able to move in six years later in 1732, although work continued until 1740. Further alterations were carried out in the 1770s by the Count's son, who succeeded his father in 1749, under the direction of the architect Filippo Castelli, who also designed the pretty oval chapel in the garden, dated 1778.

Conte Carlo was a friend of Filippo Juvarra, the great architect of the Piedmontese court, and the design of Guarene shows Baroque touches typical of Juvarra, notably the rounded corners and stepped back-garden frontage. Typically for Piedmont, brick is used throughout, for the rusticated basement, the pilasters, entablature and parapet; only the capitals are in stone, carved with the family emblem of a wheel.

The entire centre of the Castello is filled by two vast monumental spaces. A cavernous vaulted staircase hall painted with illusionistic architecture is reminiscent of Juvarra's *salone* at Stupinigi. Real windows retaining their original casements alternate with *trompe l'œil* ones painted with vistas of further halls. Beyond lies the even larger *salone* lit by three tiers of windows opening on to the garden.

The Galleria was painted in the 1770s by a local artist, Giuseppe Palladino, in a style that is still rococo, with *trompe l'œil* trelliswork opening on to a sky painted with pairs of *amorini* trailing garlands of flowers. The niches contain *grisaille* statues standing on pretend plinths. On the walls is a pretty imitation Chinese wallpaper of pink and blue flowers on a strong yellow ground. This is printed in squares but hung with the pattern dropped alternately as if in rolls. The floor is paved in tiles of two different colours laid in a zigzag pattern. This has been relaid using the original tiles, with the patterns varying from room to room. Here, as elsewhere in the house, the doors are hung with pairs of curtains (or *portières*) in fabric matching the wallpaper.

The Chinese Bedroom is a breathtaking survival. It is hung with a landscape paper which a surviving account, dated 10 June 1774, shows

was shipped by sea from London to Nice and then transported by mule to Turin – a trek of eleven days. The spirited rococo stucco on the ceiling, picked out in colours complementing the wallpapers, was executed by a stuccador from Como by the name of Bertoli in 1775. The bed is hung in bright-yellow silk, with a scalloped edge to both top and base painted to match by a Roman artist, Gregorio Guglielmi. The shallow tester above the bed is given an extra flourish by a pair of exotic urns.

Next to it is the Chinese Sitting Room, with more painted paper hangings imported from London in 1774. These wallpapers, very fashionable in England, were exported from China and backed with lining paper or canvas. Sometimes they consisted of individual scenes that were meant to be placed in frames. Here they went together to form a continuous panorama interrupted only by doors and windows. The scenes are full of humour, with figures in a garden setting against a background of spiky mountains.

The Camera Blu dates from about 1760 and is designed to provide a sense of cool in summer, with embroidered white-linen hangings to both doors and bed. The curtains on the right of the fireplace, apparently fronting a pair of matching double doors, in fact conceal nothing more than a blank stretch of wall. By contrast, the curtains to the right of the bed open into a closet taking the form of a *predagio*, or prayer chamber.

The framed wall panels are prettily painted with drapery and trailing flowers, with a Cupid's bow and quiver over the fireplace. Here, as elsewhere, the chimneyboard is painted to match the room. Miniature blue-and-white pots, probably of Turin manufacture, stand on brackets over the fireplace and doors.

The painted architecture of the dining room opens to an *al fresco* sky in which an illusion of height is created by a lozenge pattern that diminishes in size towards the centre. To ease the transformation from a square room to a ceiling on a circular pattern, the four corners are cut off with triangular squinches which allow the painters to continue their *trompe l'œil* decoration across the whole room.

The Camera del Vescovo also has a spectacular state bed with embroidered hangings and matching window curtains and furniture covers, and grotesque ornament in the style of Jean Bérain on the walls and vault. Inset into the walls of this room is a series of landscapes on canvases in raised frames painted in imitation of pinky-grey marble. The paintings are by the Milanese artist Angelo Maria Crivelli and Pietro Domenico Oliviero, who worked in the Palazzo Reale in Turin. The furniture in the Castello, although French in style, is of Piedmontese make.

Guarene remained in the Roero family until 1899, when, on the death of Conte Alessandro, it passed to the family of Provana di Collegno. Recently Guarene has been opened to visitors on the last three Sundays of September and the first two Sundays of October. Various events are held in the summer concluding with a concert under the stars when the garden is lit by torches.

Above: *The dining room. The oval portrait of Conte Giacinto Roero faces the one of his wife across the room, while the overdoors portray scenes of the hunt.*

Right: *The Chinese Sitting Room. The pretty rococo ceiling plasterwork is painted in naturalistic colours.*

TWO

VILLA TORRIGIANI

TUSCANY

The Villa Torrigiani boasts the stateliest approach of all the Lucca villas: a magnificent avenue of mature cypresses some 750 yards in length aligned directly on the entrance front. The avenue emerges at a little *borgo*, a cluster of humble estate cottages laid out to form a small piazza outside the gates. To the left, the village chapel, with its Baroque façade and Romanesque campanile, closes the vista. By contrast, the entrance gates are a bravura display of Baroque swagger, with columns deeply imprisoned in bands of rusticated stone and already visible at a distance.

Early in the seventeenth century, the villa was acquired from the powerful Buonvisi family by Marchese Nicolao Santini, ambassador of the Republic of Lucca to the court of Louis XIV. He remodelled the sixteenth-century Buonvisi villa, adding another storey and dramatically enriching the entrance front.

The architect was almost certainly Muzio Oddi (1569–1639) from Urbino. In 1625, Oddi was entrusted with responsibility for Lucca's city walls, to which he added a magnificent series of bastions.

Lucca was at that time the capital of an independent republic, but even then it was most renowned for the aristocratic villas built on surrounding hills. 'Lucca does not furnish large squares, wide streets or magnificent palaces,' Peter Beckford observed in his *Familiar Letters from Italy*, written in 1787. Instead, he said visitors should 'see the beautiful villas Santini and Mansi', repeating a saying of Samuel Johnson about David Garrick's villa on the Thames that 'these are the things that make a *death bed horrible*'.

Most Lucca villas have two principal fronts: the façade *a valle* looking to the south and the valley below, and the façade *a monte* to the north. The façade *a valle* at Torrigiani is stylistically on the cusp between Mannerism and Baroque. The characteristics of Mannerism are complexity, ornateness and a sophisticated play on the grammar of Classical architecture. Instead of the giant porticos with which Palladio graced his villas, here one loggia is set above another. Both are in the manner of triumphal arches, with a large central arch flanked by smaller openings. The same grouping is repeated in the windows on either side. In his *Italian Journey* of 1581, Montaigne noted that these loggias were a special character-istic of Lucca villas and town palaces: 'The gentlemen of Lucca eat in public in summer, under these entries in sight of anyone passing along the street.' Mannerist, too, is the contrast of colours and textures – rough yellow volcanic tufa combined with smooth-cut grey stone and set off by low-relief panels of white marble. The elaborate treatment continues within the loggias, where walls and ceilings are broken into an elaborate pattern of panels.

An eighteenth-century plan shows Torrigiani with swirling *parterres de broderie* on both sides of the house. These were swept away early in the nineteenth century when the grounds were landscaped in the English style, but remarkably one element of the Baroque garden survives intact, the *giardino segreto*, or sunken garden, to the east of the house. Vincenzo Marchio, in his *Strangers' Guide to Lucca* (1720), wrote of many villas 'famous for the wealth of gardens, avenues, labyrinths, fish ponds, grottos, fountains, water games, theatres and buildings fitted with various statues'. This could be a description of the *giardino segreto*, which is laid out on a geometrical plan with edgings of box. It is approached down matching flights of balustraded steps, which can be drenched

Preceding pages (left): *The great avenue of cypresses leading to the villa. The original late-sixteenth-century house was remodelled for the Santini family in the second quarter of the seventeenth century to the designs of the architect Muzio Oddi.*
(right): *Contrasting colour and texture create complex patterns, mixing tufa, smooth-cut ashlar and white marble.*

Right: *The* salone. *The large canvases are by Vincenzo Dandini, the eighteenth-century ceiling frescoes by Pietro Scorzini.*

with jets of water just as visitors descend. At the far end is a delightful octagonal domed pavilion, known as the *ninfeo*. Inside, this is a wonderful example of grotto architecture, eaten away by constantly dripping water. White marble statues personify the winds. The god Aeolus, master of the winds, is recognisable by his crown. Instead of the more usual four winds here there are seven, the eighth side forming the entrance. They include Boreas, an old man, for the north wind, and Zephyr, the mild west wind. Between the niches containing the statues are herms standing on scroll pedestals, all much eroded. By contrast, the mosaic frieze, inset with scallop shells at the angles, is still crisp. The pebble mosaic floor is laid in a pattern of arabesques.

Walls and floor are fitted with more hidden water jets, designed to surprise and entrap visitors as soon as they are inside. It is contrived so that there is just one spot that remains dry.

Left: *The first-floor loggia has painted decoration attributed to Scorzini. Busts of Roman emperors stand on scroll pedestals.*

Below: *The* giardino segreto, *a wonderfully preserved seventeenth-century sunken garden.*

Further jets flood the steps leading up to the roof terrace on the *ninfeo* where the cupola is cooled by waters splashing down from the top.

These water games entertained adult visitors as much as they do children today. There is a delightful account of the French writer Charles de Brosses becoming so excited by the *scherzi d'acque* at Frascati that he was drenched again and again, returning to his inn after each fresh soaking until his entire wardrobe was saturated. At Torrigiani a plentiful supply of water is ensured by a large storage basin a mile up the hillside.

The principal room inside the villa is the *salone*, which runs through the centre of the house, from front to back, like the characteristic *portego* in a Venetian palace. The long walls are inset with two large canvases by Vincenzo Dandini (1607–75), brother of the better-known Cesare. The subjects are *Aurelius triumphing over Queen Zenobbia of Palmyra* and *The Battle of the Romans against the Amazons*, a double billing of *femmes fortes*.

The room is decorated in a sumptuous Baroque manner, freely mixing two- and three-dimensional ornament. The scrollwork around the paintings makes the most voluptuous of picture frames,

threaded through with trails of gilt flowers. A gilt background further highlights the ornament of pilasters and capitals, contrasting with the bronze tones of painted trophies between. The ceiling is the work of the Lucca painter Pietro Scorzini and is a splendid example of *quadratura* – the use of foreshortening to create the illusion of a soaring architectural space above. The theme is *The Apotheosis of Aureliano*, suggesting that the Santini, like many Roman families, traced their descent from Marcus Aurelius. Scorzini also painted several other rooms in the villa.

The staircases in the villa are compact and inconspicuous. A plan dating from before the seventeenth-century remodelling shows long flights of steps, presumably enclosed in typical Renaissance tunnel vaults. The present elliptical staircases, rising around narrow open wells, were presumably introduced during the remodelling. In Italy they are known as staircases *a lumaca* – slug-shaped and gracefully cantilevered from the wall. On the half-landing is a *grisaille* of a niche within a niche, akin to those on the main front. The walls of the vestibule leading to the stairs are also frescoed with *trompe l'œil* architectural perspectives.

The main rooms are arranged in two sets of apartments, on both the *piano nobile* and the floor above, with each room opening into the next. Most of these rooms have deeply coved ceilings with frescoes by Pietro Scorzini. The dadoes are painted in *trompe l'œil*, mostly in imitation of panelling. The treatment is different in almost every room: the dado in the main bedroom is painted to look like marble, while an upstairs sitting room has a very pretty trelliswork dado. In some rooms tricks are played even in the reveals or 'cheeks' of the window by painting them with vistas of further windows. The only three-dimensional decorative elements in many rooms are the cornice and the doorcases, which are executed in *scagliola*. None of the principal rooms have fire-places, suggesting that the villa was rarely used in winter months. Instead, the rooms all have glazed tiles set in a diamond pattern, the coolest form of flooring in the heat of the summer.

A splendid state bed with hanging tester survives in the principal bedroom. As is characteristic of Italian beds of this type, the bed itself has a scallop-topped base responding to the curvilinear tester, with bold Baroque urns at the corners filled with decorative flower arrangements.

The print room over the portico on the north side is closely hung with topographical views in gilt frames; the upper row runs like a continuous frieze. The open beams are painted with trailing vines,

with insets imitating coloured marbles and allegorical scenes in the panels. The surprise of the house is to find an untouched Baroque theatre cleverly contrived within the eaves of the roof. The stage benefits from the extra height of the belvedere on the roof. Spectators watched from a shallow auditorium and balcony above. The proscenium arch is decorated with military trophies and a shield bearing the Santini coat of arms. The hooped arrangement of the rafters suggests that there was originally a barrel vault over the little auditorium. The theatre apparently retained all its stage equipment until early in the twentieth century; fortunately, the painted wings have survived. The positioning of the theatre at the top of the house comes as a surprise but is paralleled at the Château de Brissac on the River Loire.

In the Marchese Mozzorosa's 1843 *Guida da Lucca* the Villa Torrigiani is described as 'the Queen of all the Lucca villas. The house has three vast stately stories and every convenience for a numerous staff with basements for the offices so that it appears the home of a sovereign rather than a private citizen.' He also notes the groups of trees planted 'a few years ago' – this was presumably when the ornamental parterres on both sides of the house were grassed over. Today the planting is mature, a mixture of conifers and deciduous trees which nonetheless respects the central axis, leading the eye directly up the hillside from the portico.

It was at around this time that Lucca and its villas began to be discovered by the English. The Old Pretender had stayed at Lucca for a while in the early eighteenth century – his Manifesto was issued from Lucca – and in 1818 Shelley took the Casa Buonvisi, where Byron stayed for several weeks. Where Byron went, the English followed, and according to *The Story of Lucca* (1912) by Janet Ross, 'a whole population of Britons took up abode here in the first half of the nineteenth century'.

The aristocratic government of Lucca was suppressed by Napoleon, but the Santini family continued in possession of the villa. The last to live there was Nicolao di Cesare, who died in 1816. He had been ambassador of the Republic to the King of Naples and was survived by two daughters. The second, Vittoria, married Pietro Guadagni, Marchese Torrigiani.

Above: *The statues inside the* ninfeo *personify the Winds. The inlaid pebble floor conceals trick water spouts.*

Right: *The water jets in action on the steps leading down to the sunken garden.*

THREE

VILLA PIZZO

LAKE COMO

The dulcet quality of villa life on Lake Como has been praised since Classical times. Pliny the Elder talks of his villa on Lake Como in his famous *Natural History*, while Pliny the Younger, writing to Caninus Rufus around the turn of the first century AD asks: 'How is that sweet Comum of ours looking? What about the most enticing of villas, the portico where it is one perpetual spring?' He continues to extol 'the sunny bathroom, those dining rooms for large parties, and the others for small ones, and all the elegant apartments for repose, both at noon and night.' Just across the lake from the site of Pliny's villa is Pizzo, at one of the best vantage points of the whole lake. The hills around Lake Como rise so steeply from the shore that there are few places that are not in deep shadow for much of the morning or afternoon.

Pizzo, because it stands on a point or spit – hence its name – basks in the sun the whole day long. The lake is wide enough to allow the morning sun to strike early while the opposite eastern shore lies in the shadow of mountains that climb some 3,000 feet almost sheer behind, and in the afternoon the sun sinks gently into a declivity behind Chiasso on the Swiss border. The beauty of Pizzo lies not only in the marvellous views it commands up and down the lake, but also in the lushly planted gardens which run undisturbed for at least half a mile along the shore.

The name Pizzo first appears on an act of sale of the estate from Pietro Raimondi to Giovanni Muggiasca, a merchant of Como, dated 9 July 1435. The Muggiasca family built here not a villa but a simple *casa di campagna* – referred to in the will of Nicolao Muggiasca as a '*casa di padrone*'. Then, in 1630, the year of the Great Plague in Como, the Muggiascas took in a large number of refugees from the city and set them to work terracing the hillside for vines and olives.

Although much remodelled in the eighteenth and nineteenth centuries, the form of the house today appears to date from the sixteenth century. Like many Lombard villas, it is built against the hillside, with access at different levels on the land and lakesides. The main entrance opens, unusually, directly on to a grand staircase, one flight leading up to the apartments on the *piano nobile*, the other down to the apartments on the lake. Internally the principal features dating from this early period are the open-beam ceilings, prettily painted with arabesques in blues and blackcurrant, and the massive stone chimneypiece in the upstairs library.

Early in the eighteenth century, the Muggiascas commissioned a splendid series of painted friezes in the main rooms. These are of such remarkable quality, so lively and colourful, that they have on occasion been attributed to Tiepolo and Carlone. Another possible candidate is Sebastiano Galleoti, a Florentine painter who worked around Turin and Vicenza. This type of broad frieze, with strong architectural elements in the form of fragments of entablature, is relatively common in Lombard villas. With the frescoes in the library it is difficult to conceive that they can have been painted without a knowledge of Tiepolo's great ceiling in the Palazzo Clerici in Milan, executed in 1740. The satyrs in particular recall Tiepolo's ceiling. Other possible authors are the brothers Galliardi. One, Giovanni Antonio, would paint the *quadratura* or architectural illusion, the other, Bernardino, executed the figures.

During the eighteenth century, two of the Muggiascas were prominent figures in the Church: the Abbot Gian Francesco, who built a chapel next to the house – later remodelled in Neo-Classical

Preceding pages (left): *The Villa Pizzo, seen from the lake. The gardens extend along the lake for more than half a mile. A small sixteenth-century house built for the Muggiascas, a Como merchant family, it was enlarged in the eighteenth century.*
(right): *Looking along the garden terrace to the* villetta.

Right: *The Empire-style saloon with its ornamental terrazzo floor and* trompe l'œil *ceiling.*

style – and the Monsignor Giambattista Muggiasca, who became Bishop of Como in 1765. It was probably the bishop who commissioned the frescoes in the vault of the lower hall, which, though Neo-Classical, have strong Baroque elements, suggesting they may date from the 1770s.

The last member of the Muggiasca family, Giovanni Battista, was responsible for the downstairs saloon, a superb example of Empire decoration executed in chaste greys and yellows – all the material for the curtains and chairs shown here was remade, following the originals, in the late 1950s. The room has an exceptionally fine terrazzo floor with a central motif of acroteria. The ceiling is exquisitely painted in *grisaille*, suggesting beautifully carved coffers and ribs. The central mirror on the left wall, with highlights of gold, echoes the door surrounds. In front of it stands a console table resting on winged sphinxes.

Above: The library, with frescoes inspired by Tiepolo's great ceiling in the Palazzo Clerici, Milan.

Left: Detail of a frieze in an upstairs bedroom 'in the manner of Ricci'.

During the 1820s or 1830s, the Muggiascas divided up the rooms on the eastern side of the house into smaller apartments. The ceilings were frescoed and the Marchesa's bedroom was painted with the simulated coffering at this time.

On the death of Giovanni Battista Muggiasca in 1842, the whole property was left to the hospital at Como. It quickly caught the eye of the Archduke Ranieri, the Austrian Viceroy of Lombardy and the Veneto. He already had an official country residence at the Villa Reale at Monza, but by this time summer social life was gravitating to Lake Como. The exiled Queen Caroline of England had acquired the Villa d'Este. Although charitable property in Italy has by law to be sold at auction, Ranieri was able, in the Italian phrase, to secure it 'behind closed doors'.

Ranieri left his principal mark in the gardens. As head gardener, he brought in Ettore Villoresi, an educated figure who spoke both Greek and Latin and had an extensive knowledge of plants and garden design. The English style of naturalistic planting had first been advocated in Italy in 1808 by Conte Ercole Silva, and the gardens, previously formed of terraces of olives and grapes, were laid out with winding paths, no less than 14 miles in length

according to one estimate. These paths ascend in five levels from the house, interconnecting so that it is never necessary to take the same route twice. The views as you rise from level to level become increasingly spectacular, with terraces at vantage points.

In 1848, the year of revolutions all over Europe, the Austrians were driven from Italy, and, although they returned, Ranieri himself never came back. Instead, following the abdication of the Austrian Emperor Ferdinand I, the new Emperor Franz Josef, on whom so many hopes rested, decided to send his brother Maximilian to Lombardy as Governor. Maximilian was instructed to win the loyalty of the Lombard nobility and held a court of exceptional splendour. For two summers Maximilian and his young bride, Princess Carlotta of Belgium, came to Pizzo. That Pizzo held a very special place in both their memories is evident from a letter Carlotta wrote ten years later, when her husband had begun his ill-fated term as Emperor of Mexico and the spectre of assassination was already looming: 'I never cease thinking of you, my darling, everything here speaks of you. Your Lake Como of which you were so fond, lies before my eyes, so calm and blue.'

After the War of Independence in 1865, Pizzo was acquired by Madame Musard, the wife of the musician Alfredo Musard, who was the son of the more famous Philippe, formerly a conductor at the Drury Lane and Lyceum Theatres in London. If less talented than his father, Alfredo was equally successful with concerts in Paris, and his pretty young wife, promenading in the Bois de Boulogne, caught the eye of King William III of Holland. She

became his mistress – he was not to marry until later – and to further their liaison the King helped her acquire Pizzo. Madame Musard promptly set about adding her own touches to Pizzo, painting the ochre walls a shade of rose and adding curious but amusing hats to the chimneys with bells that tinkle in the breeze.

In 1871, Madame Musard left the Villa and the property was acquired by the Volpi Bassani family. They built a large boathouse at the far end of the gardens with a terrace overlooking the lake – in all, there were no less than thirty-two boats at Pizzo, including motorboats, rowing boats, sailing boats – and the Archduke Ranieri's caique, which still survives.

Pizzo was put into immaculate order by the daughter of Sandro Volpi Bassani, the late Marchesa d'Amico, and her husband. The Marchesa was a frequent visitor to England and had many English friends. Pizzo during the summer was the scene of many house parties and the gardens along the lake and the myriad paths and walks were opened to their full extent. The beauty of waking up to the view of the lake with steep wooded hills rising on the far shore and the still water echoing to the sound of church carillons was unsurpassed. The Marchesa was very fond of a game she called 'botchets', played on a billiard table without cues. Pizzo remains in the ownership of her family.

Above (left): The ante-room, frescoed during the 1830s or 1840s; (right): The Marchesa's bedroom.

Right: The lower hall, frescoed in around 1770.

FOUR

PALAZZO ALBRIZZI

VENICE

More splendid aristocratic palaces survive in Venice than in any city in the world, dominating the Grand Canal and numerous piazzas around the city. Others are tucked away along alleys and minor canals, like the Palazzo Albrizzi, which overlooks a small *campiello* not far from the Campo S. Polo.

The Palazzo has belonged to the Albrizzi family since the seventeenth century, and its principal glory is the splendid apartment on the *piano nobile*, dating from around 1690–1710, which has some of the most sumptuous and spirited Baroque plasterwork to be found anywhere in Europe. Baroque artists delighted in the art of illusion, of creating theatrical effects, of bringing buildings and interiors alive with a sense of movement, or indeed by freezing movement as if in a photograph.

Numerous palaces in Italy are peopled with gods and goddesses, angels, cherubs and playful *amorini* floating across walls and ceilings. In the Albrizzi they take on three-dimensional form, no longer confined within the bounds of a frame but hovering freely. The climax comes in the ballroom, where twenty-eight life-size *putti* cavort regardless of the calls of gravity amid the loose folds of a tent roof. Some are struggling to emerge; others tug or pull on the fabric or cling to it. The artists have perfectly captured the fun children would have if they could fly.

As Venice was a republic, both families and historians were discouraged from glorifying individuals, and it can sometimes be hard to pinpoint which member of a family or even occasionally which branch was responsible for a particular phase of a *palazzo*'s architecture. There are fewer early descriptions of individual palaces by foreign visitors than might be expected – the result of the Republic's determination to keep Venice isolated from outside influence. 'All communication with the natives is strictly forbid,' Gibbon wrote in 1765. In 1739, Charles de Brosses found the nobles lived entirely among themselves, 'admitting strangers neither to their houses nor their parties'.

The palace was built in the sixteenth century for the Bonomi family. The Albrizzi family bought it from them in two stages, part in 1648 and part in 1692. The Albrizzi were of Bergamo origin and were raised to the nobility in 1667, twenty years before the Rezzonico family. This was at the time of the Cretan wars, which were proving a great drain on the Republic's resources; for just over twenty years, between 1646 and 1669, the Golden Book, the official register of noble families, was reopened after centuries of closure. The members of the family inscribed were Giovanni Battista (died 1710), Giuseppe (died 1726) and Alessandro (died 1716), who alone had children.

Venetian palaces are laid out with an apartment on each principal floor opening off a long gallery, known as a *portego*, which runs from front to back and is lit by windows at either end. The *portego* on the first floor of the Albrizzi is an explosion of richness with decorative plasterwork surging across walls and ceilings, bursting beyond the usual confines of carefully disciplined panelling. The scheme is developed around a series of large canvases set into the walls with stucco picture frames more flamboyant and elaborate than any in carved wood. Typical of the Baroque love of metamorphosis is the way the scrollwork sprouts into large fronds of foliage which entwine themselves through the bolection moulding around the picture and gracefully interlace between the pairs of large canvases in the centre of the walls.

Preceding pages (left and right): The ballroom houses one of the most remarkable tableaux vivants ever conceived, with twenty-eight putti cavorting across the ceiling regardless of the laws of gravity.

Right: The characteristically long Venetian portego on the first floor which runs from one side of the palace to the other. The plasterwork, dating from the 1690s, is attributed to the Ticenese Abbondio Stazio.

At the top of each painting, pairs of *putti*, or rather merfolk with fishtails, wrestle playfully, while above them human-sized cupids and angels streak across the ceiling. Over the doors are a series of relief panels showing allegorical figures and, at the sides, trees that burst through the bounds of the picture frame.

The paintings are traditionally attributed to Pietro Liberi (1614–87), a painter of salacious nudes, but are more likely to be by a number of artists. One painting, *The Wheel of Fortune*, is now firmly attributed to Sebastiano Mazzoni. It is a play on the Albrizzi coat of arms, which displays a lion and a wheel set over a gateway. A glorious three-dimensional version of the coat of arms, complete with the winged figure of Fame trumpeting the glory of the family, is illustrated on the front endpaper of this volume. The *portego* also has a fine set of Venetian rococo armchairs and canopies ranged along the walls. The forms are more exaggerated than in French rococo, with serpentine backs and interwoven splats with *rocaille* or shellwork detail. They date from the mid-eighteenth century. The large, colourful carpet is said to be Spanish.

The boldness of the idea and the scale on which it is executed put the ceiling in a class of its own, but there are good reasons for attributing it to a Ticinese stuccador called Abbondio Stazio, who worked in Venice for a number of years. The ceiling of the Sala dei Trofi in the Palazzo Sagredo is inscribed with his name and that of his pupil Mazzetti and dated 1718. There are many parallels between the two, notably with the Sala del Alcova, now at the Metropolitan Museum in New York. There, in the ceiling above the bed, *putti* struggle with a similar curtain with an identical gilt fringe, while *putti* frolic through the air above the alcove arch. The inspiration nonetheless came ultimately from Rome, where many Ticinese plasterers went to work. The great sculptor Gianlorenzo Bernini was a pioneer of the sculptural setpiece and *tableaux vivants*. He had used the device of flying *putti* drawing back a curtain in the Sala Ducale in the Vatican, while in his church of S. Andrea del Quirinale, *putti* fly across the dome free of the bounds of any frame.

The Music Room is a Venetian version of Louis XVI, with tall rectangular mirrors quite in contrast to the riot of curves in the Baroque rooms. The beauty comes partly from the unusual proportions: a shallow dado no higher than the backs of the diminutive chairs topped by the very tall mirrors in slender frames, with even more slender dividers allowing the mirrors to be larger than the broadest sheets of glass then available. The beauty of this room also lies in its colouring. The misted silver of the mirrors contrasts with the glint of the gilding and the faded satin brocade of the chairs and settees.

The Albrizzi family, who continue to live in the Palazzo, came from Bergamo in the seventeenth century. Appropriately for the creators of a tent roof in stucco, they had been merchants in canvas as well as becoming involved in the Levantine trade in oil. The most notable member of the family was the poetess Isabella Albrizzi, who Byron called the 'de Staël of Venice'.

From the *campiello* outside, the house may lack external show, faced as it is with render rather than stone. This may be because most visitors approached not through the maze of narrow alleys but by water on one of the two narrow canals, the rio di San Cassiano and the rio della Madonetta, which lead directly to the palace from the Grand Canal. Thus they would have entered through the impressive water gate and up the steep barrel-vaulted staircase rising to the *piano nobile*.

The walled garden of the palace, approached romantically across a bridge over the canal and entered from the apartment on the *piano nobile*, was once the site of one of the numerous private theatres in the city, the Teatro di San Cassiano, built in 1636.

The repeating floor plans of Venetian palaces makes them very suitable for apartment living, sometimes with different generations living on different floors and the low-ceilinged mezzanine or attic floors offering rooms of cosier proportions that are easier to heat in winter. By contrast, the rooms of principal apartments have neither fireplaces nor stoves – to which they owe in substantial part their perfect state of preservation. The pattern of identical apartments on different floors can be traced back at least to the fifteenth century and is found at the famous Ca d'Oro on the Grand Canal.

A special beauty of Venetian palaces lies in their terrazzo floors, which are often as old as the rooms. The sheen on their surface provides a watery reflection of sunlight, particularly in the great windows that fill the end of the *portegos*, that is entirely appropriate in a city long celebrated as the Queen of the Lagoon.

Above: *The Red Saloon with typically exotic Venetian rococo furniture.*

Right: *The Music Room. The chairs and settees, still covered in their original satin brocade, are Venetian Louis XVI.*

FIVE

VILLA LECHI

BRESCIA

On the landing of the main staircase of the Villa Lechi is a simple marble tablet commemorating Napoleon's visit in 1805.
It concludes with the ringing words: 'The Lechi family – For such a guest – Exultant'. Napoleon stayed for the two nights of 13 and 14
June, and came with a dazzling retinue: Marshals Bertier, Bessières, Mortier, Brune and Moncey; Generals Duroc, Caulaincourt,
Caffarelli, Bertrand, Savary, Rapp, Houtoun, Le-France and Macon.
Napoleon's reception reflects the family's close involvement in the overthrow of the Venetian Republic.
In 1797, Conte Giuseppe Lechi had marched at the head of the insurgents who took Brescia, tearing down the Lion of St Mark and
hoisting the red, white and green tricolour. Giuseppe (1766–1836) was raised to the rank of general in 1800
and later became a count of the French Empire.

His second brother, Giacomo, was a politician and revolutionary activist, but fell from favour as a result of his ideological objections to the proposed kingdom of Italy. Angelo (1769–1850), the third brother, served under Joubert and became brigade-general.

Two of the younger brothers were less martial. Bernadino (1775–1869) was a keen horticulturist and devoted himself to the family estates; Luigi (1786–1867) was a man of letters and a friend of Humboldt, the great German naturalist. Teodoro, meanwhile, served as a general in the revolutionary armies and amassed a superb collection of paintings.

In the eighteenth century, the city of Brescia was renowned for its handsome aristocratic palaces. They are the counterpart of the sixteenth-century *palazzi* in Vicenza by Palladio and his contemporaries. Lady Mary Wortley Montagu writes of one local bride who brought her husband a dowry of £3,000 a year and 'the finest palace in Brescia, far finer than any in London'. Brescia was also famous in the eighteenth century for its firearms and its silk. The Lechi family had a silk mill at S. Zeno which exported silk to England and foundries for finishing arms at Lumezzane. The Brescia nobles, unlike those of Venice, could engage in trade without losing caste.

Preceding pages (left): *The stone staircase ascending to the gallery. The lion on the handrail is a Lechi family emblem.* (right): *Twin belvederes overlook a formal garden with obelisks of holly and purple berberis hedges.*

Top: *All the architectural elements of the gallery, except the stone doorcases, are painted in* trompe l'œil.

Above: *One of the low winter rooms in the mezzanine.*

Right: *Looking from the saloon to the gallery.*

The Lechi family received the title of honourable and ancient in 1724 from the Bishop of Brescia. The property at Montirone, to the south of the city, where they built their magnificent villa, had been acquired just three years before by three brothers – Bernadino (1682–1741), Pietro (1690–1764) and the Abbot Angelo (1699–1757). Pietro, who was most closely involved, had been entrusted with important diplomatic missions, and a decree of the Venetian Senate in 1728 declared him '*publicamente benemerito*', having 'in a clever manner and often at the risk of his life defended the interests of the Republic'.

The Lechi chose as their architect Marco Antonio Turbino (1675–1756), who was descended from an ancient family that had fallen on bad times. His early works include a palace in Brescia and a villa, Il Labarinto, for the Soardi family, but from 1735 he appears to have worked almost exclusively for the Lechi family, first finishing their town palace in the Corso S. Agate in Brescia. The first payments for drawings and visits to Montirone date from 1736–38. The foundations for the villa were begun in July 1739, and by 1740 the shell of the central block was complete. By May 1741, the wooden ceilings of the *piano nobile* were installed, and work on the mezzanines was continuing in 1743. There was then a pause for ten years until 1754, when Turbino was recalled to design the wings with the chapel and stables.

The wings are set back behind the entrance front and the villa is seen to best advantage from the garden, where twin belvederes provide a view over the country around as well as the elaborate *parterres de broderie*. The deep loggia is framed by the long wings, which each have three doors, each opening into two apartments consisting of a *salottino* (used mainly for games), a bedroom, and a maid's room behind. These are in concept similar to the self-contained 'lodgings' provided in late-medieval houses in England and here served both for members of the family and guests.

The parterres are enclosed with purple berberis rather than the usual box, with clipped holly obelisks around the central pool. On one side is a *jardin potager*, on the other a bosky wooded garden with twisting walks in the English manner dating from 1820.

The main staircase emerges at a gallery entirely painted with illusionistic frescoes. This is Baroque at its most restless, with writhing pediments and tortured entablatures, not a smooth unbroken line anywhere. The illusion is completed by little painted sections of floor intended to suggest that the pedestals supporting the painted statues of gods and goddesses are three-dimensional.

The gallery opens into the double-height grand saloon or ballroom. Here, again, there is no break between walls and ceiling, which are frescoed continuously with *trompe l'œil* architecture on the boldest scale. The frescoes are the work of Carlo Carlone (1686–1775) in collaboration with Giancarlo Galli, one of the Bibiena family of stage painters, and Giacomo Lecchi of Monza.

The leitmotif of the frescoes is provided by two grand staircases which descend to the very edge of the floor. On one side, Conte Pietro Lechi descends the steps to show off his new saloon to his wife – amusingly, Carlone's signature is painted on the collar of the dog which walks ahead of them. On the other side, their two daughters stand elegantly on the landing approached by a servant bearing a tray (see frontispiece). The idea of the painted steps descending into the room compares with Tiepolo's famous frescoes in the Palazzo Labia in Venice, dated a year earlier in 1745. There, the scenes of Anthony and Cleopatra are set back behind the painted columns and arches; here, the figures seem about to step into the room. Over the (real) doors beside the stairs are *trompe l'œil* balconies painted to look as if they project into the room. The spatial tricks are completed by the stage-set perspectives of diagonally placed colonnades behind the figures of the Count and his wife – known as *scena per angolo*.

In the eighteenth century, the Lechi family would have come to the villa in June for the *villegiatura* (as the summer holiday in the country was known) and again in the hunting season from September to December. But then, as now, the villa was also used for shorter visits. While Brescia has the weather of the Alps, Montirone has that of the Appennines, and often the villa will be in full sun while a thick carpet of cloud hangs over the city.

Today, Lechi lays a geometric imprint on the landscape, extended by the quadrangular courts of stables, farm buildings and then parterres, and continued across the country in rectangular fields edged by lines of trees. Remarkably, this formality was never softened by planting in the English style.

Preceding pages: *The loggia on the garden side widens from one arch to three and then five.*

Above: *The hinges tilt the door as it opens, ensuring it does not catch on the floor.*

Right: *The stalls in the stables, set relatively close together, were for carriage horses. The Tuscan columns carry statues of gods and goddesses alternating with vases of flowers and fruit, symbolising the months of the year.*

SIX

CASTELLO DI FENIS

VAL D'AOSTA

For sheer exhilaration, there are few drives to rival the descent from the Great St Bernard pass down the Val d'Aosta on a sparkling summer morning. As the last of the mist races up the hillside, castles appear on every spur, at each twist in the valley, some only hundreds of feet above the road, others high up the mountainside. But while many command strategic points along the highway, which has existed since Roman times, Fenis instead has the enchantment of a toy fort. It stands on the slightest of outcrops with no protective ditch, and meadows lap the walls.

Certainly it boasts the full array of military architecture – encircling walls, towers, battlements, covered wall walks and bartizans – but these could never have been serious defences.

It is highly vulnerable to attack from rising ground to the south, and there is no proper system of enfilading to provide protective fire along the walls. Fenis rather belongs to the later medieval revival of interest in the trappings of chivalry, its silhouette echoing those of the châteaux in the *Très Riches Heures* of the duc de Berri.

Approaching the castle, the eye is first caught by the roofs, which glint in the sun like lead. In fact, these are the great slates found on numerous old houses in the region, laid in a diamond pattern with the lower corners slightly rounded and suggesting giant fish scales. A castle at Fenis is first mentioned in a document of 1242 as belonging to the Challant family. Gottofredo II di Challant left his property to his three nephews by a will of 1323. The eldest had entered the Church, becoming an archbishop, the second became seigneur of Ussel, some 6 miles along the valley, where he built the castle, while his brother Aimone inherited the castle of Fenis, which he rebuilt around the mid-fourteenth century. His will is dated 1377, while his wife is described as a widow in 1386. His son Bonifacio, a distinguished soldier and diplomat who led embassies to Genoa, Avignon and Paris, made important additions before his death in 1426, replacing the original small trefoil-headed windows with larger mullioned ones. At the same time, the house was extensively frescoed.

In the eighteenth and nineteenth centuries, the castle fell steadily into ruin before it was rescued by the Portuguese artist Alfredo d'Andrade (1839–1915). He spent most of his life in Italy, becoming superintendent of monuments in Piedmont and Liguria, and devoted a large part of his considerable fortune to archaeology and preservation. In 1893, he made a survey of the castle's 'truly heartrending condition' and two years later, using his own money, secured a sale. D'Andrade limited his work almost entirely to repairs and consolidation, eschewing virtually any conjectural reconstruction. A more thorough approach was adopted by the Fascists, who in 1935–42 reconstructed the *enceinte* walls with Ghibelline arrow-headed crenellations on the basis of a seventeenth-century vignette painted in a frieze within the castle. The tower inside the entrance gate was also heightened and given *mâchicoulis* and a wall walk.

The courtyard is surrounded by wooden galleries with Doric columns and Classical balustrades. These are sixteenth-century in date, although the frescoes behind are early-fifteenth-century. The ground floor is occupied with kitchens and services; the main apartments are above with a combined hall and chapel and frescoes attributed to Giacomo Jaquerio of Turin (1375–1453) or his school.

Preceding pages (left): *Sixteenth-century wooden galleries and painted decoration surrounding the courtyard.*
(right): *Both inner and outer walls are crowned by distinctive Ghibelline battlements.*

Right: *The view across the meadows to the castle, with its proliferation of towers and battlements.*

SEVEN

SCHLOSS BRÜHL

COLOGNE

Baroque sets out to stun the eye, rococo to delight it. At Schloss Brühl, both are found in intoxicating measure, with colour, richness and liveliness that are hard to match anywhere in Europe. The Schloss was built as a summer palace for the Archbishop-Elector of Cologne, Clemens August (1700–61). The Archbishops of Cologne, together with those of Mainz and Trier, were the three spiritual members of the college of nine Electors who chose the Holy Roman Emperor. From 1583 until 1761, the Electorate of Cologne was held continuously by a Wittelsbach from Bavaria – one of the reigning houses of Germany. The principal residence of the Electors was in Bonn, as Cologne was a free city of the Empire, and the Elector only had authority in criminal matters. Otherwise, his writ in the city extended only to a visit of three days.

Preceding pages (left): *The theme of the decoration of the great staircase hall is
the fame and munificence of the Elector, his high office and birth. A gilded bust of the Elector,
set on an obelisk, stands above the half-landing.*
(right): *Schloss Brühl was begun in 1725 as a summer palace for the Archbishop-Elector
of Cologne, Clemens August.*

Left: *The breathtaking staircase hall, built to the design of
the great Baroque architect Balthasar Neumann.*

Above: *Exquisite* scagliola *under the stairs. The panel inside the rich rococo cartouche
portrays the Elector's favourite sport – hunting herons with falcons.*

Clemens August succeeded his uncle, Joseph Clemens (1688–1723), as Archbishop-Elector. The choice of Joseph Clemens as Elector had been the nominal *casus belli* between Louis XIV of France and the Emperor in 1688. The Electorate of Cologne had been quickly seized by the French, but they had been driven back by Dutch and Brandenburg troops, who, to prevent a renewed occupation, had destroyed almost every fortified site in the region, including the moated medieval castle at Brühl.

In the War of the Spanish Succession (1702–14), Joseph Clemens was hardly more fortunate. He followed his brother, Maximilian Emmanuel, the Elector of Bavaria, into the French camp, and as a result had to spend twelve years in exile in France while his capital was reduced to rubble in a series of sieges including one by the Duke of Marlborough in 1703.

In 1712, Joseph Clemens began to think of rebuilding his fallen palaces and approached Robert de Cotte (1656–1739), the *premier*

Above: The Audience Chamber in the Elector's Summer Apartment. The superb rococo ceiling was designed by the great François de Cuvilliés.

Left: The Gartensaal, mirroring the proportions of the great staircase, has frescoes by Carlo Carlone and stucco trophies by Carlo Pietro Morsegno, with delightful groups of putti *blasting forth on trumpets.*

architecte of the French King, for plans to rebuild first his palace at Bonn and then those at Brühl and Poppelsdorf. Joseph Clemens' first idea was to make Brühl a 'simple *maison de campagne*'. However, in a letter of 5 May 1715, he explains that 'having visited the walls, I found that they were so strong that it would cost much more to demolish them than to build a new château' and instructed de Cotte to incorporate as much of the old *Schloss* in the new house as possible. His ideas for the approach were rather grander; there was to be an avenue all the way to Bonn, some 12 miles away, and a canal linking the moat to the Rhine so he could embark on the river front of his *Residenz* in Bonn and arrive at Brühl by water. So much reconstruction was needed to his palaces that the task of resurrecting Brühl was only undertaken by his nephew.

The young Clemens August had been sent to Rome aged fifteen and studied under the personal supervision of Pope Clement IX. Although only twenty-three when he succeeded as Archbishop-Elector, he already held the powerful bishoprics of Munster and Paderborn. The climax of his career came with his election as Grand Master of the Teutonic Order. Clemens August further enriched his treasury with a series of treaties, changing allegiance so many times that he earned the soubriquet of '*vrai girouette*'.

In turn, France, Austria, Holland and England all paid handsome sums for his support, which were invested in his many building projects.

Clemens August was a passionate huntsman, and his greatest pleasure lay in taking his falcons in search of the herons which bred in the marshy banks of the Rhine. These were found most plentifully just to the east of Brühl. The first plans for the Schloss were drawn up by Guillaume Hauberat, who had been sent to the Court at Bonn by de Cotte at the request of his uncle. Hauberat's designs were too French for Clemens August's taste, and in 1724 he replaced him with a Westphalian architect, Joseph Conrad Schlaun.

Schlaun retained the moated layout but opened up the courtyard to the east. Clemens August laid the foundation stone in 1725, and three years later the structural work was complete. In that year, 1728, Clemens August paid a visit to his brother, the Elector of Bavaria, in Munich and this resulted in a dramatic change of plan. Here, Clemens August had seen the ravishing work of François de Cuvilliés, the Court dwarf with a spark divine, who had become Court Architect in Munich in 1725. Cuvilliés introduced rococo in its most dazzling form, and although his masterpiece – the silvered

interior of the Amalienburg – was not under way until 1734, he had already decorated apartments in the *Residenz* at Munich.

On his return, Clemens August promptly dispensed with Schlaun and appointed Cuvilliés in his place. Cuvilliés filled in the moat on three sides, and placed the two principal apartments of the Elector in the south wing, overlooking the new gardens designed by Dominique Girard, who also came from Munich. Cuvilliés' first work was the Gelbes Appartement, with very fine rococo plasterwork by Johann Peter Castrelli. He also designed the exquisitely decorated hunting lodge nearby, Schloss Falkenlust, begun in 1729 and completed in 1740.

The 1740s brought another complete change of plan. Schlaun had designed an open carriageway through the centre of the house, allowing guests to dismount from their carriages under cover. To the south, he had designed a spacious stair leading directly to the Elector's apartments on the first floor. Clemens August now

Right: *The Chinese Lacquer Cabinet in Schloss Falkenlust, a small hunting lodge in the grounds of Schloss Brühl, designed by Cuvilliés.*

Below: *The Cordoba Leather Room in the north wing of the Schloss. On the right, the Elector is portrayed in blue hunting dress with one of his falcons.*

decided to replace this. One reason was that Schlaun had not provided sufficient space for the preliminary ceremonials. Clemens August's Court ordinances of 1726 laid down that on state occasions, members of the Court were to await visitors in four different places according to their rank – at the bottom of the stair, in the *Gartensaal* (the equivalent of the French *salle des gardes*), in the *Rittterstube* (knights' hall), or in the *Antekammer*, an anteroom to the audience chamber.

To achieve the overwhelming magnificence he desired, Clemens August turned to the great Balthasar Neumann (1687–1753), creator of the stupendous staircases at Schloss Bruchsal, the Vienna Hofburg and the Würzburg Residenz. The staircase at Brühl is a place to make a choir burst spontaneously into song. *Scagliola* provides colour more ravishing than the most exquisite marble, colour that has the intensity of precious stones: deep blues and a strong pink below, above a green that is only a touch less intense than malachite, culminating in a pinky mauve splashed with yellow. Combined with a creamy white that is as blemishless as the finest Carrara marble, the whole hall glows thanks to the extraordinary sheen on the surface of the *scagliola*. The life-size stucco figures by Giuseppi Artari are as graceful and handsome, as noble and distinct in character as the gods and goddesses in Tiepolo's great ceiling frescoes at Würzburg.

The theme of the decoration, it need hardly be said, is the fame, the power, the munificence, the good taste, the high birth and high office of Clemens August. The eye is drawn to the gilded bust of the Elector, set on an obelisk to further trumpet his fame and placed at the same point as the bust of Louis XIV on the Escalier des Ambassadeurs at Versailles. Faith and Justice are seated on the columns above, while below are Nobility and, rather incongruously, Modesty. At either end stand two figures of Fame, one with the Elector's coat of arms, the other with his initials. Over the doors are the symbols of his high offices, as Bishop, Legatus Natus, Elector and Grand Master; above are portraits of the four previous Wittelsbach Electors of Cologne. Crowning it all, glimpsed through a huge oval balcony, is Carlo Carlone's fresco of Magnanimity and Munificence as Benefactresses of the Arts. Here,

Above: A Bavarian porcelain stove in the Summer Apartment, made in Bavaria to the design of Cuvilliés. The blue-and-white chequer pattern of the dado is the emblem of the Wittelsbach family.

Left: Blue tiles create a feeling of cool in the summer dining room at Schloss Brühl. The peasant scenes are after engravings by David Teniers.

another obelisk emblazoned with the Elector's initials soars into the sky, while on the shield of Munificence a ground plan is engraved lest we forget that the fame of princes is secured through great works of architecture. Further sparkle is provided by the richly decorative gilt ironwork of the staircase balustrades by Johann Georg Sandtener. The sheer theatrical splendour and inventiveness of the whole composition now appears to be due, even more than to Neumann, to Johann Anton Biarelli, a designer at the Bonn Court.

The ceremonial that accompanied a state visit to Brühl is conveyed in the report of the Abbé de Guébriand, the ambassador of Louis XV, who arrived for an audience at the Schloss on 21 November 1747. After he had passed the officers of the Court ranged in the hall, 'the chief equerry received me at the doors of the first chamber, the grand marshal at the second, and the grand marshal, in the absence of the great chamberlain at the third'.

The south wing contains both Summer and Winter Apartments. All these rooms have rococo ceilings with flowing ornament, two of the finest being the Audience Chamber of the Summer Apartment and the *singeries* ceiling in the Winter Apartment (reproduced on the rear endpaper of this book), with playful monkeys cavorting in a celestial world of trellis and flowers. Lady Mary Coke, who spent a day at Brühl in 1767, exclaimed: 'The ceilings of two or three of the rooms are beyond any of those the King of France has at Versailles; they told me they had cost the late Elector forty thousand florins each.' The ceiling plasterwork of the Audience Chamber is by Artari himself, with a swirling richness that sweeps up the straight lines of the cornice with scenes of hunts by Joseph Billieux.

No visit to Brühl is complete without an excursion to Falkenlust, which offers a world of enchantment akin to the Amalienburg in the grounds of the summer palace of Nymphenburg at Munich. Falkenlust, as its name suggests, is a hymn to the falcon and combines the charm and style of banqueting house and *pavillon de plaisance*. Here Clemens August relaxes just a little, indulging in the same rapturous beauty of décor but on a more intimate scale. Appropriately he is painted in what might be taken for the most luxuriant of all dressing gowns in the portrait over the fireplace in the exquisite black-and-gold Chinese Lacquer Cabinet.

Following damage suffered in the Second World War, Brühl was meticulously restored and is now open to the public and much used for state occasions.

EIGHT

SCHLOSS FAVORITE

BADEN-BADEN

Numerous German princelings sought to build a Marly as well as a Versailles and gave them names such as Monrepos, Solitude, Monbijou, Belvedere and Sanssouci. These more intimate summer retreats, always full of charm, vary from small banqueting houses or pavilions, intended for an afternoon's dalliance, to great country palaces, such as those the Archbishop-Electors of Cologne built at Brühl and the Palatinate Electors established at Schwetzingen.

Schloss Favorite lies between these two extremes. It was close enough to the capital of Rastatt for the Margraves of Baden-Baden to visit in a day, but large enough to house a substantial Court. It is the creation of Sibylla Augusta, who for twenty years after the death of her husband, best known as Louis the Turk, acted as both Dowager and Regent.

Over the next twenty years, she did much to restore the shattered fortunes of the principality with the help of her neighbour, the Prince Bishop of Speyer at Bruchsal, and the vast revenues from her own estates. Like her husband she had the *Bauwurm* (the building bug) which infected so many German rulers, building the Schlosskirche and Pagodenberg at Rastatt and rebuilding the Schloss at Ettlingen.

Her first move at Favorite was to dismiss Rossi as Court architect and import her compatriot Michael Ludwig Rohrer (1683–1732), a pupil of the great Bohemian Baroque architect Christoph Dientzenhofer. In around 1710, during a long stay in Bohemia, she drew up plans for a *Lustschloss* (a pleasure palace) modelled on Schloss Schlackenwert, her family's principal estate near Karlsbad. For Favorite, she chose a site midway between the old and new capitals of the principality, in a flat stretch of farmland just below the first slopes of the Black Forest hills. As at Versailles, a level site was evidently the perfect canvas for large formal gardens.

Work began in 1710 and the roof was on by the winter of the next year, completing what in Germany is called the *Rohbau* – the shell. The charm of the house lies in the details, such as the delightful pinched architraves over the first-floor windows.

From 1543 onwards, there had been two Baden principalities on the Rhine: the Catholic Margraves of Baden-Baden and the Protestant Margraves of Baden-Durlach. After the devastation of the Thirty Years War (1618–48), the area was ravaged again by the French following Louis XIV's invasion in 1688. Baden-Baden suffered severely because Margrave Ludwig Wilhelm was fighting the Turks on the eastern frontier of the Empire and every *Schloss* in the state was destroyed by French troops.

Ludwig Wilhelm's successes led the Emperor to arrange for him to marry one of the richest heiresses of the Empire, Princess Sibylla Augusta of Saxe-Lauenburg. Orphaned at the age of fifteen, Sibylla Augusta shared the enormous family estates in Bohemia with her elder sister, who married the last Medici Grand Duke of Tuscany.

For the first years of her marriage she followed her husband from camp to camp on his campaigns against the French. When peace came, Ludwig decided to forsake the old capital and *Schloss* at Baden-Baden and commissioned the Italian architect D. E. Rossi to build a new *Residenz* at Rastatt (which survived the Second World War largely undamaged and is now open to the public). In 1707, soon after the main structure was completed, Ludwig died of an incurable war wound, leaving Sibylla Augusta as Regent for their five-year-old son.

Preceding pages (left): *The sala terrena, faced in blue-and-white tiles to create a feeling of a cool summer hall.*
(right): *The garden front, seen across the lake, was created in the nineteenth century when the park was landscaped in the English style.*

Above (left): *A pietra dura panel in the Florentine Room;*
(right): *A panel of beadwork in the Audience Chamber.*

Right: *The Florentine Room is lined with decorative panels inlaid with mother-of-pearl, agate, onyx and marble. The design of the floor is as elaborate as the ceiling.*

Left: The Margravine's bedroom. The canopied state bed is set in a raised alcove. Doors on either side opened into closets and provided access for servants.

Above: The family drawing room. The raised bandwork ornament is decorated with sprays of flowers cut out of silk.

The façades are covered with a coating of pebbles and granite chippings – the mother of all pebbledash, and the first indication of the Margravine's interest in unusual decorative techniques and materials. By tradition, the pebbles were collected by local children from a nearby river, the Murg.

The house is planned around a central *sala terrena*, a cool summer room of the type found in Italian villas from the sixteenth century onwards. The walls are faced in blue tiles, made in Nuremberg in imitation of the more familiar Delft tiles, which portray country scenes. The architectural trim is executed in *scagliola*, cleverly imitating rich red, yellow and brown marble. The glaze of the tiles and the sheen of the *scagliola* create an instant sense of cool. With water trickling over the shells beneath the statues, it made a perfect summer dining room. Galleries at first-floor level link the two sides of the house, while a central octagonal cupola allows light to descend from above. When the doors were

folded back, the *sala terrena* also acted as a porte-cochère, with carriages driving in one side and out the other. Internal windows at first-floor level also heightened the courtyard feel.

The principal apartments are on the *piano nobile* – on one side those of the Margravine, on the other those of her son. In place of traditional wall coverings such as tapestries, damask, paintings or stucco ornament, the Margravine experimented with a whole range of decorative techniques and unusual materials: papier mâché, pasteboard, painting on parchment and *pietra dura*, the latter presumably supplied by her sister in Florence. Sibylla Augusta evidently had a horror of bare walls that led her to embroider every surface with a pattern.

The first room of the Margravine's apartments is decorated with elaborate borders of ribbonwork, inspired by the engravings of Jean Bérain, whose work epitomises the *Régence* period in France, between the Baroque of Louis XIV and the rococo of Louis XV. The ribbonwork is made of green and gold papier mâché built up in complex geometric patterns, and interlaced with flowers made of silk and the fine fabric known as batiste. All these have been renewed with consummate artistry following surviving traces of the original. Doors and doorways are faced in beautifully matched veneers, with the grain running in horizontal or slanting bands. The parquetry floors are also inlaid on geometric patterns varying from room to room. As they were in bad condition, they have been remade in the same four woods as were used originally – oak, cherry, nut and maple.

The Margrave's apartment on the other side of the house includes a study hung with squares of Chinese wallpaper and the Florentine Room. This is one of the most richly treated of the exotic curiosity *cabinets* in which German rulers delighted. The centre of each wall consists of a trellis-pattern mirror with a miniature portrait painted on each diamond-shaped pane of looking glass. In all, there are 150 portraits taken from Sandrart's *German Academy*. The walls around are inset with over five hundred small panels of inlay in mother-of-pearl, marble intaglio and *pietra dura* of harbours and hunting scenes and mythological figures. Numerous marbles and semi-precious stones are used, including lapis lazuli, agate, onyx and alabaster. Around the mirrors are panels of coloured stucco flowers, while the dado is painted in imitation of Chinese lacquer. The extraordinary *scagliola* floor is executed in delicate pinks and blues. *Trompe l'œil* details prompt the visitor into stooping to pick up playing cards, quills, sheets of paper, insects – even a whole chessboard.

The Mirror Cabinet is inset with over three hundred mirrors of different sizes and shapes, often at strange angles. It is also inset with a series of small parchment panels painted with figures of the Margravine, her husband and children in costume. She appears as shepherdess, Baden peasant, huntress, Roxana and Tartar. In the window reveals, there is a gallery of famous beauties.

In the Margravine's bedroom, the bed is set on a raised dais and framed by a proscenium arch and balustrades. In the corners of the ceiling, *amorini* hold mirrors as well as shields with the arms of Baden-Baden and Saxe-Lauenberg over the arch. The *scagliola* floor is designed to look as if it is made of panels of real marble, laid in geometric shapes. The walls are covered in rich damask.

Sibylla Augusta compiled a book of recipes of decorative techniques, such as painting on agate. In the Audience Chamber there are panels of needlework vases of flowers, executed in pearl stitch, the thread being strung with small coloured glass beads.

A picture of life at the Margravine's Court is provided in the memoirs of the Baron de Pöllnitz, who arrived at Rastatt in February 1730 and, as was his custom, immediately sought an audience with Sibylla Augusta and her son. To his chagrin, this was not granted, but after looking round the *Residenz* he fell into conversation with a courtier who told him that the Margravine 'had introduc'd into her Court the Ceremonial of the Eastern Princes; that she never appear'd but in a full Divan and that she did not permit any one whatsoever to come near to her Son except the Bashaws and Dervizes who were of the Council'. When Pöllnitz ventured that he had heard the Margravine was 'very much of a Christian, not to say a heroine', the courtier continued, 'The Margravine has Piety and Virtues … but she has a Haughtiness, and a certain *Particularity* in her Temper … if she had receiv'd you, it would have been standing under a Canopy by an Arm-Chair, with as much State as the Empress'. Usually, he said, she dined in private and was hardly seen except at mass.

The four square knights' houses (*Kavalierhauschen*) south of the Schloss suggest that the Court moved here in summer, at least in part. By contrast, the Hermitage in the wood shows the value Sibylla Augusta placed on solitude. This was a sanctuary where the Margravine took refuge to do penance – 'Pity for the great sinner' was carved on her gravestone. This is a small octagonal building clad entirely in bark with a series of very small rooms ranged around a central chapel. The Margravine would prepare simple meals for herself in the kitchen and eat them in the dining room beside life-size wax figures of the Holy Family.

The Margravine's son, known as Jäger Louis for his love of hunting, rarely came to Favorite, and following his brother's death the Margravate merged with that of Baden-Durlach. In 1803, Napoleon created the Grand Duchy of Baden with the capital at Karlsruhe. The Grand Dukes built the Neues Schloss at Baden-Baden, but Schloss Favorite continued as a summer residence and early in the nineteenth century the formal layout of canals was swept away to create an English park and lake. When Germany became a republic at the end of the First World War, Favorite went to the State and is now owned and run by the Land of Baden-Württemberg, with exemplary care and scholarship.

Above: The enfilade through the Margravine's apartments, showing the inlaid parquet floors.

Right: The Mirror Cabinet, inset with dozens of mirrors in walls and ceiling set at angles to provide multiple reflections. Small pictures painted on parchment portray the Margravine as shepherdess, Baden peasant, huntress and Tartar.

NINE

SCHLOSS WEIKERSHEIM

WÜRTTEMBERG

Weikersheim shows German Renaissance architecture at its most proud and ambitious. Soon after 1586, the Dutch architect
Georg Robin planned a new castle in the form of an equilateral triangle for Count Wolfgang of Hohenlohe.
Although only one wing was executed, it contains one of the grandest Renaissance halls in Germany. Its survival is all the more remarkable
as the Hohenlohe line here was Protestant and in 1634 the town of Weikersheim was ransacked by Imperial troops and
the county ceded to the Order of Teutonic Knights. Their *Schloss* at Bad Mergentheim is only 5 miles away.
The Hohenlohes astutely recovered Weikersheim at the Treaty of Westphalia in 1648 and went on to embellish the Schloss
with Baroque interiors.

Then, in 1756, the castle passed to another branch of the family, and for nearly two centuries Weikersheim was only occasionally used – hence there were no Neo-Classical or Victorian alterations destroying earlier work. It was not until 1945, following the loss of the Hohenlohe estates in Bohemia and Yugoslavia, that a member of the family, Prince Constantin of Hohenlohe-Langenburg, moved back. His first concern was to conserve the character of the Schloss, and over the next three decades he put the castle and grounds into immaculate condition, leaving little obvious trace of his work. The result is a castle-museum full of atmosphere and interest without any attempt at a lived-in look, but where the visitor steps back in time as soon as he begins to mount the castle stairs.

Preceding pages (left): The Mirror Cabinet of 1708–17, with the original Chinese porcelain set on small gilt brackets.
(right): The garden front, completed in 1603, with triangular gables reflecting the intended triangular plan of the Schloss. The fountain portrays Hercules wrestling with the Hydra.

Top: *Looking out on the great parterre, designed by Daniel Matthieu.*

Above: *The Knights' Hall, conceived as a celebration of the chase.*

Right: *Sculpted animals in the Knights' Hall include deer with real antlers.*

Today, the country around Weikersheim is known proudly as Hohenloheland after a series of castles including Schloss Neuenstein and Schloss Langenburg. Both are open to the public. Geographically, Weikersheim lies at the north-east extremity of Swabia, now the rich modern state of Baden-Württemberg, but the people here consider themselves Franconians, not Swabians. Traditionally, they have looked north to Würzburg, rather than south to Stuttgart, and their line of communication has been with the Rhine and ultimately with Amsterdam rather than Switzerland and Italy.

Robin entrusted the supervision of the building work in 1595 to Wolf Beringer, a master builder he had worked with at Würzburg. Building work came to a halt after the south wing had been completed, but a further range facing the town, known as the Langenburg Wing, was added to the design of Paul Platz in 1679–84.

Although Weikersheim was the *Stammschloss* and principal residence of Count Wolfgang, it served chiefly as a great hunting lodge. Württemberg was astonishingly rich in game of every kind. The chase forms the leitmotif for the Knights' Hall, which is dramatically decorated with life-like sculptures of stags ranged along the upper walls. The smaller deer, such as the chamois, are grouped in twos and threes, in wonderfully active poses, at one end of the hall. Progressing down the room, the animals become steadily larger and pairs give way to single beasts, including a splendidly ferocious bear, with a lion and an elephant forming the climax.

The animals were modelled by Gerhard Schmidt, who was brought from Königsberg in Prussia, and his assistant Christoph Limmerich. The naturalistic colouring of the animals was the work of a local man, Caspar Dietrich. The bodies of the deer are made of chalk and animal hair rather than plaster and carry real antlers. Such verisimilitude was not to be achieved until the advent of taxidermy.

The ceiling canvases were painted by Balthazar Katzenberger, a Würzburg artist, and portray hunting for elk, heron, boars, lions, elephants and even crayfish, showing netting and shooting at night with the aid of torches and drums. The magnificent triple-decker chimneypiece, by Michael Junker and his sons Hans and Zacharias, carries the arms of Count Wolfgang and his wife, Magdalena of Nassau-Katzenelnbogen, sister of the Dutch monarch William the Silent. From the reclining figures of the Count and Countess spring two family trees, each with a full array of sixty-four aristocratic quarterings. The panelled dado, inset with painted views of castles and gardens, is an early-eighteenth-century introduction.

Weikersheim contains a spectacular series of state beds. The Blue Bed, dating from 1711, has lion's-head feet and a rich acanthus and shell cresting to both bed and canopy. In the centre of each side is a phoenix, the emblem of the Hohenlohes. The bed retains its original silk-damask drapery, and beside it sits a cradle made for the Prince's heir in 1716, the year of his birth, by J. H. Vogt.

A vivid picture of the glory of sleeping in these beds is provided by Tatiana Metternich in *Five Passports in a Shifting Europe*, describing her flight from the Russians in 1945. At Weikersheim, 'the four poster bed was prepared for us: silky smooth sheets, and pillows piled high, and edged with white laced flounces'. A shell had blown out the window but the weather was warm and 'as we lay in the great state bed, under its Lyon-velvet, scalloped canopy, we gazed past faded crimson hangings straight into moonlit fields'.

The Mirror Cabinet at Weikersheim deserves comparison with that at Schloss Favorite and is virtually contemporary, dating from 1708–17. It is the work of Johann Jakob Sommer and his sons Philipp Jakob and Georg Christoph. The mirrors are very small, some being roundels no larger than the palm of a hand, though slightly larger ones, like ladies' hand looking glasses, are placed at angles. The room served as a display cabinet for dozens of tiny pieces of Chinese eighteenth-century porcelain, both vases and figures, which remain balanced on the miniature brackets and shelves designed to support them. In contrast to the rococo chinoiserie *cabinets* of the mid-eighteenth century, none of the decorative detail is Chinese but consists of bandwork and gilded

scrolls of acanthus. The present red-silk background was introduced by Prince Constantin.

The great Baroque parterres outside the Schloss were laid out by the Frenchman Daniel Matthieu, the Saarbrucken Court gardener. The garden is also rich in sculpture, with a delightful series of dwarfs. The central fountain contains a group of Hercules fighting the Hydra surrounded by figures of the four elements, the four seasons and various gods. These and other sculptures were executed by Johann Jakob Sommer and his sons in 1708–24.

Weikersheim is remarkable in Germany for the survival of so much furniture and so many decorative *objets d'art*. While many of the great German *Schlösser* lost their contents when they were expropriated at the end of the First World War, Weikersheim passed with its contents to the Land of Baden-Württemberg on the death of Prince Constantin.

Above: *The triple-decker chimneypiece in the Knights' Hall, dated 1602. On either side of it, the reclining figures of Count Wolfgang and his wife sprout family trees displaying their noble ancestry.*

Right: *The carved and gilt Baroque state bed of 1711, showing the phoenix emblem of the Hohenlohes.*

TEN

PEACOCK ISLAND

BERLIN

Follies have long been enchanting features of the parks and gardens of great houses.
On Peacock Island, the Prussian kings went a step further, creating an Elysium that consisted entirely of small buildings, eyecatchers,
temples, simulated ruins, peasant cottages and native huts.
When guidebooks proclaim that Berlin is a green city, this is due in impressive measure to the Prussian kings,
who in the late eighteenth century and early nineteenth century turned their minds from drill and discipline to extend the gardens
around Potsdam in the south-west from one palace to another, forming a continuous composition in which woods, hills,
lakes and islands all played a part.

Frederick the Great began with Sanssouci, and his successors continued with landscaped grounds of Glienicke and Babelsberg. To the north of Potsdam, the New Gardens – with the Marmorpalais on the water's edge – were created by Frederick William II, who succeeded Frederick the Great in 1786. From here, he went boating on the Havel, a large lake where the *Pfauen Insel*, or Peacock Island, offered the perfect goal for his excursions.

The island at this time was in a wild state and the King chose to leave it so. Although prehistoric remains have been found in recent decades, the island is first recorded only in 1683. Two years later, Frederick William, Elector of Brandenburg, gave it to the chemist Johannes Kunckel, famous for his development of artificial rubies,

who used it for his experiments in glass manufacture. Just over a century later, in 1793, Frederick William acquired the island from the orphanage that owned it. The King first camped here in an oriental tent, quickly embarking on a series of buildings beginning with the *Schlosschen*, or Little Schloss.

Within four years, he was dead of the dropsy and his son Frederick William III continued the work. He was influenced by François Quesnay, who argued that land and its products were the only true source of wealth: he built a cattle stall, followed by a farmhouse. Around his dairy, rye potatoes, oats and clover were already growing in 1799, while four years later there were thirty-five head of cattle, three buffalo, forty-eight sheep, and two goats.

With the peace of 1815 a new mood came to Berlin: more lighthearted, more artistic, with a taste for the exotic. Peacock Island was transformed by Peter Josef Lenné, the greatest German landscape gardener of the age. He introduced sinuous paths, clumps, groves and belts in the English manner, with carefully planned vistas at every bend. To obtain a proper grass sward, an Englishman named Humphreys, director of the Potsdam-Magdeburg Steamship Company, was summoned in 1822–24 to install a steam engine to pump water from the Havel to a tank at

Preceding pages (left): The Little Schloss, a piece of pure caprice without any attempt at a veneer of antiquity. It was built in 1794–96 for the Prussian King Frederick William II by Johann Gottlieb Brendel, the Court carpenter. (right): The Kavalierhaus, remodelled by Schinkel in 1823 to incorporate the façade of a Gothic house from Danzig.

Above: The Festsaal in the Little Schloss, with walls and floor inlaid in exotic woods.

Right: The Tahiti Room, inspired by the voyages of Captain Cook, is painted in simulation of a native hut with panoramic views over palm-fringed islands.

the highest point of the island. From here, it was distributed by underground pipes.

Lenné's planting, though English in character, included a wide variety of ornamental trees as well as the hardwoods of English parks. The fields disappeared, though the animals remained as Peacock Island developed along the lines of the Jardin des Plantes in Paris, with a growing variety of zoological and botanical specimens. An inventory of the Royal Menagerie dated 31 May 1842, shortly after the death of Frederick William III, includes an ape house, a kangaroo house, a sheep stall, a llama house, a bear pit, a wolf kennel, a wild-boar stall, an eagle house, a volary, a duck pond, a pheasantry and a badger house.

There was a rose garden with three thousand plants and the Fouchiron collection of large and rare palms housed in a large palm house built in 1831, which alas burnt out in 1880. Delight in the exotic and oriental did not stop at buildings and animals; the island also boasted human specimens. These included a Sandwich islander, Heinrich Wilhelm Maitey, who arrived on Peacock Island in 1830, and a Negro, Karl Ferdinand Theobald Ilissa. There were also a giant and a pygmy brother and sister. Johann Gottfried Schadow describes the arrival of a group of artists on Peacock Island in August 1825. They watched as 'monkeys like acrobats turned somersaults' and gazed at motionless owls 'with eyes glowing like Egyptian idols'.

The high point of a visit was the Little Schloss, with two toy-castle towers linked by an arched bridge. According to the Royal Inspector of Works, Kruger, the design was the King's 'very own idea'. Inside, wall hangings and wallpapers survive virtually unfaded. In the corner tower is the Tahiti Room, painted by Peter Ludwig Lütke. This is designed to look like the interior of a bamboo hut, with panoramic views over palm-fringed islands. The carefully knotted reeds of the painted roof form a perfect pattern of diminishing squares, like the coffering of a Classical dome. Balustrades are formed of bamboo trellis, with reeds and creepers apparently growing immediately outside the windows. Grohmann's *Ideenmagazin für Liebhaber von Garten* (a major source of ideas for garden ornament in Germany) included a design for a Tahitian hut in 1799.

The use of simulated architecture continues with the staircase, where the walls are painted with rusticated quoins in yellow and grey and the shadows vary according to the way the light would fall. The cantilevered staircase rises to a small landing at first-floor level and then continues in an unbroken flight of fifty-two steps, creating a corkscrew effect emphasised by the spiral of the handrail.

The *Festsaal* on the first floor takes up the entire width of the Schloss. This is a highly original room where the decoration of walls and ceiling is carried out entirely in inlaid wood – veneers of elm, nut, black poplar, plum apple and chestnut. The pilasters are in burr walnut, while the veneer facing the wall behind is straight-grained like silk. This chastely Neo-Classical room dates from 1790 and was executed by Johanne F. Selle and Johann Christian Ziedrich, with carved detail by Johann Christian Angermann. In character, the *Festsaal* has much in common with the Etrurian Cabinet in the vanished *Stadtschloss* in Potsdam, designed only slightly later by Gottfried Schadow for Frederick William III.

The fireplace in this room, like all the others in the Schloss, is of a distinctive spherical shape, on the pattern developed by the American adventurer Count Rumford, who entered the service of the Elector of Bavaria. He had produced an authoritative study on fireplaces and was renowned for curing smoking chimneys. The use of open fireplaces is in contrast to the normal German preference for stoves. Two of the upstairs rooms in the Schloss retain their original Indian chintzes and have wallpaper surmounted by resplendent peacocks. A number of wallpapers complete with borders survive, made at the factory of J. Christian in Berlin.

The Dairy, designed by the Court carpenter Brendel, is a sham ruin containing a delightful *trompe l'œil* Gothic room on the first floor by the painter Verona, who received a fee of 450 thaler. The Gothic detail relates to Gothic buildings shown in a painting by Schinkel. The original furniture, with its pretty interlacing backs, survives.

The *Kavalierhaus* in the centre of the island was built in 1802 as a farmhouse but remodelled in 1824–26 by Schinkel to incorporate the façade of a late-medieval house from the Brotbänkengasse in Danzig. Today, Peacock Island is looked after by the Prussian State Administration of Castles.

Above: *Looking up the well of the cantilevered spiral stair in the Little Schloss. The painted coffering adds to the swirling movement.*

Left: *The first-floor room in the Dairy, with deliciously exotic painted Gothic decoration.*

SCHLOSS EMKENDORF

SCHLESWIG-HOLSTEIN

The English Prime Minister Lord Palmerston famously remarked that only three people understood the Schleswig-Holstein question.
One was himself, and he had forgotten about it. The second was Bismarck, and he was dead.
The third was a German professor, and he had gone mad thinking about it. Although the two duchies were for centuries part of the
kingdom of Denmark, the aristocracy had strong links with Germany and in 1848 the province was annexed by Prussia.
Like the villas of the Veneto or the Quintas of the Douro, the country houses of Schleswig-Holstein – known as *Herrenhäuser* –
are built on a distinct pattern. 'The châteaux of this duchy,' Horace Marryat wrote of Holstein in his *Residence in Jutland* (1860)
'are all constructed on a single plan … round a large court … in front stands the *Schloss*, a large substantial edifice …
flanked by two enormous buildings with high-pitched roofs, each one the dimensions of the abbey church at Malvern.'

At Emkendorf, the public road running past the house is planted with a stately avenue of chestnuts and limes, giving it the character of a private drive. As it approaches the house, the road makes a sudden loop as if to pass at a respectful distance. The *avant-cour* is flanked first by matching ranges of L-shaped stables, each with a pilastered centrepiece in the manner of a triumphal arch, and then by two characteristically massive barns. 'The size of the cow-houses,' wrote Samuel Laing in his *Notes on Denmark and the Duchies* (1851), 'and of the barns which hold all the winter provender for 240 cows, (for the corn and hay crops are under roof, and nothing is stacked out of doors,) is prodigious.' At Emkendorf,

the barns lie end-on rather than parallel but nevertheless add a strong processional element to the approach.

Emkendorf today is above all the creation of Count Fritz Reventlow, who inherited the estate in 1786, and his wife Julia. From 1650 to 1720, Emkendorf belonged to the powerful Rantzau family, who sold the estate to Melusina von der Schulenburg (1667–1743), Duchess of Kendal and the mistress of George I of England (nicknamed the Maypole by the London populace). The Duchess was insatiably acquisitive, but she sold Emkendorf in 1729, two years after George I's death, and retired to live at Kendal House at Isleworth, on the River Thames.

The estate was then acquired by the Hanoverian field marshal Freiherr C. J. von Bülow, but was sold in 1738 by his son to W. H. von Baudissin, general and cabinet minister. He in turn sold the estate to Graf J. H. des Mercières, who received the Danish King here in 1748.

The newly married Reventlows had visited Rome in 1783–84, and two years later the young Count had been appointed Danish ambassador to London. Sophie de la Roche describes a visit to the Reventlows' London house in 1786: 'there are some fine souvenirs of her Italian trip, evidence of her good taste. The Count and

Preceding pages (left): *Rococo plasterwork survives above the later ceiling of the Neo-Classical* Festsaal.
(right): *The Schloss seen from the stable court. The huge symmetrically placed barns are typical of the* Herrenhäuser *of Schleswig-Holstein. On the left is the cow house of 1730; on the right, the grain barn of 1745.*

Above: *The first-floor* Festsaal, *with Neo-Classical decoration inspired by Raphael's Vatican loggias.*

Right: *The Etruscan Room. Its colour scheme is inspired by Greek vases, which appear in a* trompe l'œil *vignette above the stove.*

Countess had copies and pictures made by artists of the great masters' finest paintings and of the loveliest spots they came across.'

The Count began to remodel the existing rococo Schloss in 1791, to the designs of Carl Gottlob Horn (1734–1807). In 1795–97, the Reventlows spent a further two years in Rome and brought back a young decorative painter, Guiseppe Anselmo Luigi Pellicia. He was not to begin work until 1802, when a large crate of paintings from Rome, intended for incorporation into decorative schemes, at last arrived. The best of Pellicia's work is in the *Festsaal* on the first floor, evidently inspired by the Raphael loggias in the Vatican, with the walls arranged as a series of piers with separately treated doors or arches between. Over the fireplace is a splendid copy of Guido Reni's painting of the Archangel Michael in the church of Santa Maria della Concezione in Rome. Other paintings dwell on the theme of Love: two roundels in the ceiling depict Jupiter and Io, and Narcissus and Echo.

Next door is the Etruscan Room, painted in shades of brown, emulating the colouring of Greek vases, with a *trompe l'œil* painting of a group of vases over the stove. A letter from Reventlow to his brother mentions that Pellicia made no drawings but worked directly on the walls and ceilings.

Some of the plaster ceilings, executed by the Italian Francesco Antonio Taddei, have patterns very similar to ceilings by Adam and others in England. Interestingly, the subscribers to

Richardson's *Book of Ceilings* (1778) include one of Reventlow's predecessors as ambassador to London, Baron Deide de Furstenstein.

Family correspondence, including exchanges with the architect, shows there was a clear division in function between the ground floor and the first floor. The Count and Countess both had their apartments on the ground floor. The state rooms and principal apartments for guests were on the first floor. The Count's apartment, to the left of the entrance hall, set the tone with a combination of decorative painting and inset canvases of very high quality.

The oils over the doors, with languid figures portraying the four seasons, suggest the name of Angelica Kauffman or her circle. In the Adlerzimmer on the ground floor is a large oil of startling quality by the French painter François-Xavier Fabre of Venus and Adonis, after architect Carl Gottlob Horn.

The house remained with the Reventlows' descendants until 1926, and three years later it was acquired by Dr Curt Heinrich, whose son Freiherr von Lüttwitz Heinrich embarked on a careful programme of conservation that has continued ever since.

Above left and right: *Neo-Classical stoves in the* Festsaal *and the first-floor library – unlike stoves in some German castles, these are fed from the front rather than the passage behind.*

Right: *Count Reventlow's bedroom. The overdoors portray the four seasons; the* grisaille *friezes are revels of Bacchus and Dionysus.*

TWELVE

SCHLOSS STOLZENFELS

RHINELAND-PALATINATE

'The several communes which owned old ruined castles on the Rhine,' wrote the Duchess de Dino as she sailed down the river in 1843, 'have presented them to different princes of the house of Prussia: thus apart from Stolzenfels, which belongs to the King, and Rheinstein which belongs to Prince Frederick, the Prince of Prussia has received a castle, as also has Prince Charles, and even the Queen has her own. They are all on the left bank and the King has ordered the new owners to restore them and make them habitable.'

Frederick William IV, who succeeded his father as King of Prussia in 1840, had been enraptured with the Rhine on a visit in 1815, immediately after the Rhine provinces had been ceded to Prussia by the Congress of Vienna. 'On passing all those thousand divine castles and cliffs and mountains and currents,' he wrote with romantic hyperbole, 'I was weary with bliss.'

Although the Prussian Court is associated principally with the great series of Neo-Classical buildings in Berlin, designed by Schinkel and others, Frederick William's interest in Gothic architecture is demonstrated in a portrait with the Gothic canopies of the chapel of the Berlin *Schloss* in the background. The choice of Gothic may also have been influenced by a desire to identify with the liberal reforms of the Whig aristocracy in England, as with certain nineteenth-century castles in Bohemia, such as Lednice. On his accession, the new King relaxed press censorship, extended religious freedom and promised a central constitution; but later in his reign, *Rundbogenstil* (round-arched or Romanesque style) was favoured precisely because it was free from the liberal associations of Gothic.

Stolzenfels was originally built for the Archbishop of Trier, Arnold von Isenburg (1242–59), and was used for the Rhine toll levied on shipping. In around 1400, substantial additions were made, probably under Archbishop Werner (1388–1418), including the tall castle keep. During the Thirty Years War, the castle was taken and retaken by the French and Swedes, and it was burnt by the French in 1688 during their unsuccessful siege of nearby Koblenz.

In 1802, the ruin passed into the possession of the City of Koblenz and, according to Dumas *père* in his description of the Rhine, was put on sale for ten Louis 'without arising the interest of any traveller in acquiring it'. In 1823, the town therefore made a gift of Stolzenfels to the Crown Prince, who, in Dumas's words, was '*parfaitement artiste et homme de goût*'.

Frederick William promptly commissioned the Koblenz architect Johann Claudius von Lassaulx to survey the ruin and produce a plan for its reconstruction as a royal residence. These plans were sent to Schinkel in Berlin, but no work was carried out, and in 1834, the Crown Prince was considering the transformation of the castle into a landscaped ruin. But the following year he sought new plans from Schinkel, stipulating that 'the remains should as far as possible be preserved, and a new building erected on the old foundations corresponding with the needs of the present day'. No difference between the old and the new stonework was to be visible.

The Gothic Revival began later in Germany than in England. Its first stirrings are marked by Goethe's essay *Von Deutschen Baukunst* in 1772. Goethe, his imagination fired by Strasbourg Cathedral, argued that Gothic architecture was a German creation. Others followed, including Ludwig Tieck, who speculated 'perhaps we shall one day discover that all the splendid buildings of this kind

in England, Spain and France were created by German masters'. Yet the first Gothic Revival buildings in Germany show strong signs of English influence. Stolzenfels, as reconstructed, is very much an essay in English Tudor Gothic as practised by Repton and Nash. In composition it follows closely the remarks on castles in Humphry Repton's *Theory and Practice of Landscape Gardening* of 1816. Repton's great principle 'on which the picturesque effect of all Gothic edifices must depend' was 'irregularity of outline; first at the top by towers; secondly … by breaking the horizontal lines with windows of different forms and heights; and lastly, by the building being placed on the ground on different levels'.

At Stolzenfels, Schinkel originally planned only to partially restore the outer castle walls, but in the event the outer defences were also reconstructed. The castle garden is within the walls and there is only one way in or out: across the drawbridge. Outside the castle, the forest was left untamed, though a new road was constructed circling over itself on a viaduct – inspired by one of Karl Blechen's paintings of Italy. Work was almost complete on Schinkel's death, and the following year there was a formal opening with a great torchlight procession, several hundred strong, of all the workmen winding up the hill in period costume to be welcomed into the castle by the King.

In 1845, the chapel was added, to the designs of Karl Schnitzler, the officer in charge of building new barracks in Koblenz. Although dramatic, it contrasts sharply with the rest of the castle, almost as if he wished to 'correct' Schinkel's freer interpretation of the Middle Ages.

Schinkel's happiest invention is the flight of steps leading to the garden from the main courtyard. With its perspective of triple arches and airy vaults, it borrows from the vocabulary of stage design. A telescopic effect is achieved by keeping the vaults at the same level and lengthening the columns as they descend the steps.

Preceding pages (left): *Looking over the chapel with the grand sweep of the River Rhine below. The ruined medieval castle of the Archbishops of Trier was acquired by the Crown Prince of Prussia, later King Frederick William, in 1823 and reconstructed to Schinkel's designs in 1835–42.*
(right): *The castle entrance, with the keep rising behind. The battlemented walls were reconstructed, leaving only one approach.*

Above: *The spiral staircase, snaking up without a central newel post.*

Right: *The Summer Hall, a Gothic version of a sala terrena, faced with blue-and-white tiles to create a sense of cool.*

The interiors of Stolzenfels were designed to convey a romantic idea of medieval life and chivalry while providing modern comforts; although the King and Queen had separate apartments, they shared a bedroom. On the ground floor the Small Knights' Hall is painted with scenes of chivalrous virtue by Hermann Anton Stilke. Courage, loyalty, righteousness and justice, and the twin medieval themes of love and song are illustrated by scenes taken from German history, portraying King John of Bohemia, Frederick Barbarossa, Emperor Frederick II, Philip of Swabia and Geoffrey de Bouillon. These paintings are in fresco — and less stilted than contemporary work at Hohenschwangau. Germany was in advance of England in the revival of fresco; for the wall paintings at St Giles, Cheadle, Pugin had used German artists in the 1840s, while Prince Albert sent artists working on the Houses of Parliament to study with the Nazarenes in Rome.

The larger Knights' Hall has a vaulted ceiling resting on two columns, with antiquarian displays of arms on the walls and a row of drinking vessels and jugs on a shelf above the panelling suggesting suitably hearty hospitality. The staircase leading up to the royal apartments is a virtuoso corkscrew spiral with the wall cut away to reveal the drama of the descent. The Queen's Drawing Room is in muted greens and browns and golds with stencilled decoration and a blind arcade around the top of the walls. At the end on the left is a small writing room with a portière, or door curtain, to provide privacy. Hanging from the ceiling is a splendid gilt chandelier. The rooms in the King's apartments are smaller, consisting of drawing room, dressing room and study. Quite a number of the rooms retain their Gothic Revival chandeliers.

Another instance of English influence is the use of fireplaces rather than the usual German stoves, though fireplaces, to Count Rumford's design, had also been introduced at Peacock Island.

Above: *The Small Knights' Hall, painted with historical scenes evoking chivalrous virtues.*

Left: *The Queen's Drawing Room, with stencilled walls, Gothic arcading and a spectacular chandelier.*

The chimneypieces at Stolzenfels are very much Gothic versions of Classical ones, rather than the great hooded mantles that were common in the later nineteenth century. Many of the windows are inset or overhung with stained glass – much of it dating from the sixteenth or seventeenth century – a taste also very much in vogue in England, for example in the work of the stained-glass artist Thomas Willement at Davington Priory, Kent, in the 1840s.

The most attractive room in the Schloss is the Summer Hall beneath the Knights' Hall, overlooking the Rhine. This is a Gothic version of the *sala terrena*, found in eighteenth-century German castles such as Favorite (see page 60). Here, a sense of cool is provided by blue-and-white tiles and a plain white ceiling set off by gaily painted ribs. Originally, this was the castle's summer dining room.

In 1845, Queen Victoria arrived by steamer to look at the castle. She was greatly disturbed when Archduke Frederick of Austria claimed precedence over Prince Albert and was greeted by Frederick William.

After Frederick William's death, the Schloss was little used; hence its survival intact until the end of the First World War, when all the former Prussian castles were placed under central administration. After 1945, Stolzenfels was transferred to the care of the Land of Rhineland-Palatinate. Standing high above the Rhine, Stolzenfels retains its proud position, commanding a vast stretch of river and densely wooded hillside. It is not a forbidding fortress but a perfect expression of the age of the picturesque, more fairy tale than real, bristling with battlements and turrets, a perfect *tout ensemble*.

Above: *The main Knights' Hall, where the armour remains as it was originally arranged.*

Left: *The castle garden, with Schinkel's vaulted steps leading through to the main courtyard.*

SCHLOSS EGGENBERG

GRAZ

The early seventeenth century was an age of favourites. England was subject to the caprices of the Duke of Buckingham;
in France, Marie de Medici left government largely in the hands of the unscrupulous Concini.
The Empire was dominated by Wallenstein, the great general, and in its civil affairs by the remarkable Hans Ulrich von Eggenberg,
whose principal memorial is the vast Schloss he built outside the Austrian city of Graz. Carl Eduard Vehse, in his entertaining
Memoirs of the Court of Austria (1856), relates that 'the Eggenbergs were originally bankers like the Medicis,
the Fuggers, and our own Rothschilds. Ulrich and Balthazar Eggenberg were masters of the mint under the Emperor
Frederic III and used to negotiate loans for him.'

Hans Ulrich von Eggenberg, born in 1568, entered the Emperor's service in 1597 and rose with meteoric speed. In 1603, he was made president of the Hofkammer; in 1619, he accompanied Ferdinand II to his election as Emperor at Frankfurt. In the same year he received the Order of the Golden Fleece. In 1621, he became head of the Imperial Privy Council and Governor of the eastern province of Styria. The following year he was entrusted with the task of bringing home the Emperor's second bride, Eleonora Gonzaga of Mantua, and acted as the Emperor's proxy at the marriage ceremony.

A grant of 1622 bestowed on him the Lordship of Krummau in Southern Bohemia, which Vehse says contained 'at that time no less than 311 towns and villages'. In 1623, he was made a Prince of the Empire, and Krummau was created a duchy five years later. He continues: 'As Wallenstein was all powerful in the army thus was Eggenberg in the cabinet. The Prince being nearly always confined to his bed by the gout and by disorders of the stomach, Ferdinand generally caused the Privy Council to be assembled at his favourite's house; to which … a secret passage led from the Hofburg.'

Overmighty favourites who build themselves vast palaces rarely endure. Like Wolsey at Hampton Court or Fouquet at Vaux-le-Vicomte, Eggenberg fell – the same year as Wallenstein, whom he survived by only eight months, dying in 1634. This was the very moment his great Schloss was nearing completion.

Hans Ulrich was building on an ancestral site that his family had acquired in the fifteenth century. Severe in design, with four massive towers at the corners, the Schloss has been called 'the Styrian Escorial'. Hans Ulrich had made no less than three visits to Spain, and there is a close parallel in the layout of his castle with the Alcázar in Madrid, which stood on the site of the present royal palace. It was the Spanish who first developed the concept of matching apartments for king and queen, and at the Alcázar they converged on an apartment of state in the centre of the main front – as the apartments converge on a central *Saal* at Eggenberg.

The other striking feature of the layout at Eggenberg is the perfect alignment of the enfilades, which run unbroken along all four fronts. Stand in any corner and you can look in two directions to the ends of the palace. Enfilades were not a feature of the Spanish palaces: the Spanish monarchs preferred a greater degree of privacy and retirement. Equally, though enfilades were to be a great feature of Versailles (much complained of by Madame de Maintenon), there is no early-seventeenth-century French palace

Preceding pages (left): *Dating from 1625–35, Eggenberg is a rare example of a great* Schloss *built during the Thirty Years' War. The magnificent state rooms are on the second floor.*
(right): *The wall paintings in riotous rococo frames were added around 1765 by J. B. A. Raunacher.*

Right: *The* Prunksaal, *decorated in the 1680s with allegorical paintings by the Court painter Hans Adam Serenio set in bold Baroque stucco frames by Alessandrio Serenio.*

with such complete sequences of doors in alignment. Instead, the inspiration came from Italy. Already in the Palazzo Farnese (begun in 1534), there are enfilades along three of the fronts, while in the Palazzo Borghese (1590 onwards), there was a very long enfilade where the doors were set in line, even though the rooms follow the curve of the street, and the illusion of infinity was created by placing a mirror at the end.

The emblematic nature of the layout suggests Hans Ulrich himself had a strong hand in the design. The two principal *Baumeister* were Laurence van der Sype and Pietro Valnegro. As a result of Hans Ulrich's fall from grace, the interiors were only completed later.

The coats of arms contain the eagles of Gradiska, a title the family only received in 1647. Hans Ulrich's son Johann Anton died aged thirty-eight, and the vast estates passed to his two sons: Johann Seyfried (1644–1713) inherited Eggenberg; the Bohemian estates went to the eldest son, Johann Christian.

The desire of the Eggenbergs to establish a great dynasty is evident in the decoration of the Schloss – the whole complex cycle of ceiling paintings appears to be conceived to show the world was

Left: *Enfilades of perfectly aligned doors run the whole length of all four fronts of the Schloss.*

Above: *Two of the elaborate mid-eighteenth-century* cabinets, (left) *with oriental porcelain inset in the walls, and* (right) *Japanese roll-paper set into painted rococo panels flanked by European chinoiserie paintings.*

a bad place before the family's ascendancy. Moralising scenes from mythology, ancient and modern history, and the Bible continue in an unbroken sequence through the twenty-four *Prunkraüme* or state rooms – a contrast to the state apartment in the Schloss at Würzburg where the Prince Bishop, tiring of so much edifying virtue paraded before him, would have nothing more than flowers in his bedroom.

The state rooms also provide a fascinating contrast between seventeenth- and eighteenth-century taste. While the ceilings portray every kind of murder, assassination and violent death in gruesome detail, the rococo canvases on the walls consist of *fêtes galantes*, garden parties and pastoral scenes. On one wall, for example, there is a lady on a swing that is pure Fragonard; immediately above, Antipater murderously thrusts his sword at his mother's heart.

The decoration of the *Prunksaal* was conceived as a didactic programme dedicated to the education of a young prince. Johann Seyfried is portrayed entering in a chariot; below him are the symbols of the sciences which will flourish under his rule, while from the palace emerge the cardinal virtues who will watch over his start in life.

In 1938, the Schloss was acquired by the province of Styria as a music school. It suffered damage in the war from both sides but was painstakingly restored in 1945–53 and opened to the public with museum displays on other floors.

FOURTEEN

CHÂTEAU DE DAMPIERRE

ÎLE-DE-FRANCE

The first sight of Dampierre compares with that of Vaux-le-Vicomte, a breathtaking panorama in which the vast extent of the formal layout can be taken in at a single glance: gates and lodges, *avant-cour* and *cour d'honneur*, flanking wings, and finally the massive quadrangle of the Château itself, with the centre set back to create a third, more secluded inner courtyard.

Dampierre is a magnificent essay in the Grand Manner of Louis XIV's reign. Order, symmetry and a grand central axis dominate the entire composition.

To this is added the other essential ingredient of the age, geometrical sheets of water – first a balustraded moat around the Château, then canals and a vast basin the size of a lake stretching out into the distance.

The story of Dampierre begins in 1525, when the estate was acquired by Jean Duval, treasurer of François I, who built a moated château around a courtyard – recorded in Du Cerceau's *Les plus excellents bâtiments de France*. His widow sold it to the Cardinal de Lorraine, one of the main protagonists of the destructive wars of religion.

The estates passed to his nephew, Henri de Lorraine, the duc de Guise, who was brutally assassinated at Blois in 1588. His widow retired to Dampierre and the Château passed to Claude de Lorraine, who ceded it in 1655 to his wife, the ambitious Marie de Rohan, duchesse de Chevreuse, whose first husband had been the 1st duc de Luynes. In 1663, she gave Dampierre to her son by her first marriage, Louis-Charles d'Albert, 2nd duc de Luynes, who the same year renounced it in favour of his eldest son, Charles-Honoré. In him, the two dukedoms of Luynes and Chevreuse were united, and ever since the titles have been borne alternately by father and son.

In 1667, the young duc de Chevreuse, aged twenty, married Jeane-Marie-Thérèse, seventh daughter of Colbert, Louis XIV's great minister, who brought him a considerable fortune. The young Duke, Saint-Simon records, was 'endowed by nature with plenty of wit … and an aptitude for work and all forms of science'. He embarked on rebuilding the Château in around 1675, obtaining designs from Jules Hardouin Mansart, *Premier Architecte du Roi*, who was then working at Versailles and later laid out the Place Vendôme in Paris.

For all the grandeur of his new residence, the Duke led a retiring life and the Château only came sparklingly to life under his successor, who married as his second wife Marie Brulart, the widow of the duc de Charost who became *dame d'honneur* and close friend of Queen Marie Leczinska. When King Louis XV dined at Dampierre in 1749, the curtains were drawn up at the end of the meal to reveal the parterres and canals lit with fairy lights to the sound of drums, trumpets and horns.

Dampierre escaped the Revolution intact. Family tradition has it that the Duke and his family were arrested in January 1794 and taken to the Prison des Anglais. Every day, a handsome daily provision of food and game arrived from Dampierre, most of which

Preceding pages (left): *A beauty holding a lamp to light the bridge across the moat.*
(right): *The Château was built to the designs of Jules Hardouin Mansart for the duc de Chevreuse. From the hill above, the whole splendid layout can be taken in at a single glance.*

Right: *The gallery was designed by Felix Duban as a setting for Ingres's mythologies. When the painter was unable to complete his work, the Duke commissioned a statue of Minerva, recreating Phidias's masterpiece, which stood in the Parthenon.*

was sequestered by the governor of the gaol, who naturally did not wish to lose so fine a source of supply by precipitately sending his guests to the guillotine.

The dining room retains the original late-seventeenth-century panelling with a plaster frieze and cornice skilfully grained to blend in with the room. Here, the handsome mirror doors are matched by sliding shutters faced with mirrors looking exactly like windows. The first-floor chapel also retains original woodwork, though the balustrades around the altar formerly stood around the Queen's bed.

More puzzling are the gloriously ornate rococo boiseries of the *salon*. As they reach almost to the floor and lack a dado, they are thought to have been moved, possibly from a pavilion that stood romantically on an island in the lake.

The enormous Salon de La Minerve is the work of duc Honoré (1802–67), a man of vast energy and an active archaeologist and numismatist. He chose as his architect Felix Duban, a leading figure at the Ecole des Beaux-Arts. In 1839, Duban had become a member of the new *Commission des Monuments Historiques* and had been entrusted with the restoration of the royal château of Blois.

Top: *The Louis XIV boiseries in the dining room are inset with mirrors intended to create reflections from candles. The plaster frieze and cornice are grained in simulation of wood.*

Above: *The family chapel on the first floor. The balustrades that enclosed Queen Marie Leczinska's bed have become altar rails.*

Left: *The richly marbled main staircase is based on the Staircase of the Ambassadors at Versailles.*

The walls of the gallery at Dampierre are faced with pilasters in white and gold, based on Italian Renaissance designs, while the ceiling is Pompeiian, painted in reds, blacks and browns. Artists who worked on the scheme include Simart, who created the reliefs in the friezes, and Hippolyte Flandrin, who supplied the figures in the oval ceiling panels.

The room was intended as the setting of two great history paintings by Ingres. In 1839, the Duke had written to him in Rome offering the spectacular sum of 70,000 francs. Ingres accepted and suggested two subjects from Hesiod: *L'âge d'or* and *L'âge de fer*, to which the Duke agreed. Ingres wrote direct to Duban saying he wanted the paintings to be semicircular, like Raphael's *Stanze* in the Vatican, adding that he wished to paint in situ, not on canvas nor even in fresco but in oil on a special plaster.

Ingres did not arrive at Dampierre until 1843, when he made more than five hundred sketches for *L'âge d'or* and finished fifteen figures. When the Duke was first allowed to see the half-finished painting, he was distressed to find so much nudity. Ingres continued to excite artist Ary Schéffer to '*un délire d'admiration*'. Then tragedy struck. Ingres's wife died in Paris, leaving the painter

mortified. The Duke released him from the contract and commissioned Simart to recreate the famous statue of Minerva by Phidias, which had stood in the Parthenon. The design was worked out with the aid of medals in his collection, in silver gilt and gilt bronze.

At the foot of the grand staircase is a white marble statue by Cavalier of the sleeping Penelope, the wife of Ulysses, placed here as a symbol of feminine virtue. The Duke also contrived a remarkable *salon* with a statue of Louis XIII, to whom the Luynes family owed their fortune – Charles d'Albert had served as his page and had been showered with honours, offices and gifts by the young King.

Today, the ducal grandeur of Dampierre lives on, reflected equally in the family's other great house, the Château de Luynes on the Loire.

Above: *The salon, with richly carved white and gold rococo boiseries. As the wall mirrors descend below the pier tables, they were probably moved here from another room and lowered to fit the space available.*

Right: *The Salon Louis XIII, with a statue of the boy King to whom the family owed its fortune.*

FIFTEEN

CHÂTEAU DE MONTGEOFFROY

ANJOU

To most visitors, the Loire is a valley of kings, dominated by great royal châteaux, with those of their consorts and courtiers clustered close around. It is a world of regal splendour, emblazoned with salamanders and fleurs-de-lys, filled with audience chambers, banqueting halls and *salles des gardes*. Brilliant and vivid but also overwhelming, and for those who long for a château that is more intimate, still furnished and lived in, Montgeoffroy is the answer. In the broad, deep dry moat and circular towers the sense of a *château-fort* lives on, mingling with eighteenth-century elegance.

The first glimpse of the house, set at the top of a gentle slope and backed by a tall mass of trees, comes as a surprise, but once in front of the handsome spiky wrought-iron gates, the perfect precision of the approach is apparent. Here is the quintessence of the elegant French château, at once timeless and in perfect harmony with the landscape around. Steep slate roofs, tall chimneys and white stone walls are all in the grand tradition of Loire châteaux. A deep dry moat encloses a large *cour d'honneur*.

The Château took on its present appearance when it was remodelled in Neo-Classical style in 1772–75 for Louis-Georges-Erasmé, marquis de Contades and maréchal de France. His architects, the brothers Barre (best known for the beautiful château of Le Marais in the Île-de-France), preserved not only the courtyard layout of the existing Château but also the circular corner towers.

'I have always felt on seeing a château with towers at its corners a sort of respect for the owner, unknown though he be; a fine house deprived of these ornaments has never seemed to me to be more than the dwelling of a wealthy bourgeois,' wrote the bailli de Mirabeau in 1770. Precisely this sentiment must have been foremost in the mind of the maréchal and his architects in preserving so carefully the character of the old house and eschewing the balustraded parapet that would be usual around this date.

The Contades had acquired the estate in 1676 from the family of La Grandière. Gaspard-Georges Contades (1666–1735) had led a brilliant military career, serving in the wars of Louis XIV and rising to the rank of lieutenant general. His son Louis-Georges-Erasmé was to surpass him when created *maréchal* in 1758. In the War of the Austrian Succession in the 1740s, he had played a leading role in the successful sieges of Fribourg, Tournai, Ostend, Nieuport and Hulst, achieving almost at a stroke what had eluded Louis XIV and Vauban in long years of campaigning.

This success was to be reversed at the battle of Minden in 1759, where the King was to blame Contades for the defeat – though Napoleon was later to attribute it to a weak opening by the duc de Broglie. Contades was never again to take command in the field and was made Commander-in-Chief in Alsace, giving the first public ball that Marie Antoinette attended. During these later years, he was often absent from his estates and it was his son Gaspard (1726–94) who supervised the work on the Château.

The main block, the *corps-de-logis*, was raised by a storey and a pair of low flat-roofed pavilions added at the corners, linking to the wings. As in many châteaux of the eighteenth century, the entrance was not beneath the central pediment but at the end, in one of the projecting corner towers. This is in complete contrast to the contemporary Palladian villa in Italy or England, but it had the

Preceding pages (left): *The handsome wrought-iron gates are attributed to a serrurier from Angers named Mistoufflet.*
(right): *The* cour d'honneur *seen from across the dry moat.*

Left: *The boiseries of the* salon *are chastely Neo-Classical, including the pier table, but the curving forms of the chairs and sofas are still rococo.*

advantage of opening up an enfilade running the length of the
house as the visitor arrived.

The interior of Montgeoffroy reflects to a remarkable extent the
attractive picture of French châteaux drawn by Lady Holland in a
letter to her sister in 1765: 'I dined and supp'd very frequently at
their villas so that I am very *au fait* of their way of life in the
country. Their houses are in general excellent. No people have ever
studied so much or succeeded so well in enjoying all the con-
veniencies of life as the French do. There is always a large salon,
an ante-chamber and eating-room together, besides little *cabinets*.
Then above stairs you have a long gallery, out of which you go to
the various apartments, some for single people, some for *mari et
femme*.'

The disposition of furniture at Montgeoffroy can be tallied
against an inventory drawn up in August 1775, just as the house
was completed (reprinted in Pierre Verlet's *La Maison du XVIIIe
Siècle en France*). Almost all the furniture bears the marks of
leading Parisian cabinet makers, Garnier being foremost among the
ébenistes, Gourdin, Blanchard, and N.-T. Porrot among the
menuisiers. The interiors also mark the transition from the rococo of

Louis XV to the Neo-Classicism of Louis XVI, and virtually all the
rooms are painted in the pale shades of grey then so fashionable –
not just the boiseries, but the doors, the shutters and much of the
furniture. Colour is provided in the hangings and upholstery.

The *salon* stands in the centre and is highly architectural in
treatment. Five sets of double doors and blind arches, large wall
mirrors, and arches reflecting the arches of the windows leave little
space to hang pictures apart from over the mirrors.

This was a point made by the great architect Blondel in his *Cours
d'Architecture* (1771–77): 'There are some architects who, in the
decoration of apartments, make a habit of repeating false doors
either in symmetry or opposition to the real ones, with the result
that in a room where many chairs are essential some must be placed
in front of the false doors, which does not give a very natural
appearance'. Interestingly, the inventory suggests just such an

Above: *The dining room. The faïence stove in the shape of a palm tree is from
Alsace.*

Right (above): *The* maréchal*'s bed is set in an alcove crowned with military
trophies and the dove of peace;* (below): *The bedroom of Madame Herrault.*

arrangement with eighteen *fauteuils* and *chaises en cabriolet* (with curved legs and backs), eight matching *fauteuils à la Reine* (with flat backs), and four *bergères* (filled in beneath the arms), most of which are still in the room.

Dining rooms were a recent innovation in France at this date, the usual practice being to eat off moveable trestles or occasional tables wherever the family and guests were gathered. Montgeoffroy has a handsome dining room with elegantly curved ends, heated by a faïence stove in the form of a palm tree halfway along one wall and enclosed by a wrought-iron grille. The flat top presumably served as a hot plate. The only tables mentioned in the inventory are two walnut (serving) tables, which suggests that dining tables were still brought in – a total of twenty-eight chairs are listed. To the left of the *salon* is a room described in the inventory as the second ante-chamber, but which is evidently a games room, furnished then as now with tables for picquet, whist and other games.

The apartment of the maréchal leads directly out of the *salon*, consisting of a small study and bedroom where the bed is set with magnificent *éclat* in a tall alcove surmounted by military trophies. The verticality is emphasised by tall narrow panels on either side, carved with laurel wreathes.

The apartment of Madame Herrault, the companion of the maréchal in the closing years of his life, is opposite the dining room, and has rich crimson and yellow hangings of Venetian *brocatelle*. On either side of the bed alcove, the wall panels open up to reveal cleverly concealed cupboards.

The bedrooms on the first floor retain original boiseries and in some cases the original matching fabrics for walls, curtains, bed and chairs. The chairs in these rooms, unlike those below, are completely Louis XV in character, with pretty oval backs. Tall casement windows ensure that the rooms can take full advantage of the beautiful air and light in the Loire valley, making the bedrooms as pleasant to sit in as the grander rooms below.

The arrangement of bedrooms corresponds closely with that described by Lady Holland in her letter about châteaux quoted earlier. Those for *mari et femme*, she wrote, consisted 'of a little antechamber which communicates to two bedchambers, a room for each servant, and a *garderobe* for each bedchamber, sometimes a *cabinet de toilette* for madame. Those for single people were composed of a bedchamber, servant's room, and *garderobe*, and sometimes a closet besides.'

The formal layout of Montgeoffroy is a magnificent example of how the Grand Manner so beloved of the French can be applied even in a flat landscape of arable fields. From the Château the green carpet of the *cour d'honneur* is extended beyond the enclosing balustrade by sweeps of grass running gently down to the arched entrance and its distant flanking pavilions. Beyond, three diverging avenues stride outwards, proclaiming, 'All this belongs to me.'

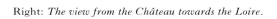
Right: *The view from the Château towards the Loire.*

SIXTEEN

CHÂTEAU DE BUSSY-RABUTIN

BURGUNDY

Louis XIV sapped the power of the French nobility by luring them to Versailles while their country estates fell into neglect.
At Bussy-Rabutin, the story unfolds in reverse, with a Count who spent seventeen years exiled to his family domains but who, far from
devoting himself to country pursuits, spent every waking moment thinking and dreaming about the life he was denied,
filling his house with portraits of Court beauties he never saw, and views of royal châteaux from which he was forever barred.
This feeling of nostalgia and melancholy is all the stronger as the house has hardly been altered since.

The medieval Château of Bussy, the property of the Chandio family, was rebuilt in the late fifteenth century as a moated *château-fort* with circular towers at the corners. Towards 1520, Antoine de Chandio remodelled the Château, demolishing the entrance range and introducing elegant Renaissance arcades along the flanking wings. These have the flattened arches typical of the transition from Gothic, as well as the panelled pilasters usual at this date. The continuous band of small windows on the upper storey, treated like a loggia, lends a particular charm. Towards the end of the sixteenth century, the Chandios fell into debt, and the house was acquired by one of their creditors, François de Rabutin, who

Preceding pages (left): *The Château stands on the moated emplacement of a fifteenth-century* château-fort.
(right): *The arcaded early Renaissance wings date from the 1520s, while the taller central block carries the date of 1649. The chapel is in the tower on the left.*

Above: *Roger de Rabutin, comte de Bussy, conceived his gallery 'as a short history ancient and modern with all I should want my children to know of the subject'.*

Right: La Tour Dorée, *'adorned with the most beautiful women in the court who have given me their portraits'. The arrangement of paintings can be confirmed by a series of surveys made for successive owners in 1781, 1806 and 1854.*

claimed it was 'on the point of falling into ruin if it was not restored immediately'. It was almost certainly he who embarked on rebuilding the central *corps-de-logis*. This is on a larger scale and in a more monumental style, with the alternating rhythms and restless façade treatment found in France during the first half of the seventeenth century. The pediments over the windows are alternately triangular and segmental, with a broken triangular pediment over the entrance and a broken segmental one above. There is hardly a stretch of plain wall to be seen: paired pilasters, Ionic below and Corinthian above, frame niches with tablets and plinths filling the wall above.

The façade bears the date 1649, suggesting it was completed by Roger de Rabutin, comte de Bussy, who succeeded his father in 1644 at the age of thirty-one. At the time he was a successful soldier with a series of distinguished campaigns behind him, as well as a succession of intrigues and quarrels which were to lead to his ruin. His first wife had died in 1646. Two years later, he abducted a very rich young widow, Madame de Miramion, having been led by her confessor to believe she wished to elope with him. Her shrieks soon proved the opposite and Bussy was forced to set her free and pay her family an indemnity of 6,000 livres. Two years later, he

remarried and with his wife's dowry was able to buy himself the rank of *mestre de camp* of the light cavalry. Almost immediately, he quarrelled with his commander, the great Turenne, and was soon in such dire financial straits that he was forced to dissolve his regiment.

During Holy Week, he and a group of fellow libertines composed a series of obscene alleluias and satirical sketches of leading women at Court. The story reached the King and Bussy was forced to retire to his Château where he developed the sketches into *L'Histoire amoureuse des Galles*. When this began to circulate, the Prince de Condé, one of the 'heroes' of Bussy's narrative, determined on his downfall and commissioned a sequel, purporting to be from Bussy's hand, satirising Louis XIV's affair with Madame de la Vallière. Bussy was cast into the Bastille and only allowed out thirteen months later, in desperate need of medical treatment.

Now in exile, he set about the decoration of his Château. The drum-like Tour Dorée is a superbly preserved seventeenth-century decorative scheme, with paintings inset into elaborate gilt frames and filling every inch of wall and ceiling. The lowest tier consists of allegories of love, with the Rape of Europa alluding to Bussy's failed abduction, and a portrait of Pygmalion with the legend: 'If you wish to love and not to be deceived love a woman of ivory.' Above is a circle of Court beauties, with amusing if hardly kind inscriptions. Catherine d'Angennes is described as 'less famous for her beauty than the use she made of it' and the Marquise de la Baume as 'the prettiest mistress in the kingdom and the most lovable if she was not also the most unfaithful'.

Bussy has belonged to the State since 1929.

Above: *La Salle des Devises, filled with views of royal châteaux and allegorical panels satirising Bussy's mistress, Madame de Montglat.*

Right: *Bussy's bedroom, hung with more portraits of Court beauties.*

SEVENTEEN

CHÂTEAU DE MEILLANT

BERRY

Meillant is an extravaganza. Here is medieval romantic fantasy in its final, most exuberant flowering, bringing to life the fairy-tale silhouettes of châteaux in illuminated manuscripts. The late medieval love of pageantry and display, the delight in the trappings of war and chivalry, even though defence against assault was no longer the primary aim, are everywhere apparent in a wealth of *armes parlantes*, bannerets and fleurs-de-lys. The plumber's art provides a profusion of lead finials, weathervanes and ornamental roof cresting. Within the Château the romance is continued in a series of colourful Gothic Revival interiors, splendidly in sympathy with the original work.

No less fantastic is the stone carving: dormer windows carrying precarious superstructures of filigree carving, superb openwork balustrades along the parapets, and gargoyles punctuating every crevice and extremity. Yet amid the frenzy of Flamboyant Gothic are the first soundings of the Renaissance: shell-headed niches, columns, ovolo mouldings, a dome and a cupola.

Meillant stands in the heart of France, in wooded country 15 miles to the south of Bourges. Its complex descent over eight centuries has always been by blood or by marriage. A château belonging to the Charenton family is recorded in the eleventh century. In 1233, the property passed to Louis I de Sancerre. Etienne de Sancerre is thought to have rebuilt the Château shortly before he died in 1308, and the south wall of his *enceinte* survives, looking out over the moat. In plan, the Château was an irregular polygon with high walls and towers, like nearby Ainay-le-Vieil today. At the end of the fourteenth century, Meillant passed by marriage to Jean de Bueil. On his death, it descended through his daughter Anne to her husband, Pierre d'Amboise, and thus to one of the great families of late-medieval France.

Pierre d'Amboise had seventeen children, while his son Jean had a further sixteen. The greatest of Pierre's children was Cardinal Georges I d'Amboise, first minister of King Louis XII of France. At one time, he held high hopes of succeeding Pope Alexander VI, but Giuliano della Rovere had been elected instead as Julius II. Among his brothers were Pierre, Bishop of Poitiers, Louis I, Bishop of Albi, Jacques, Abbot of Cluny, Jean, Bishop of Langres, Aimery, Grand Master of Rhodes, and Charles, owner of Meillant and Chaumont on the River Loire, who died in 1481. This Charles, known as Charles I d'Amboise, had taken up arms against King Louis XI and his château at Chaumont had been levelled in punishment. However, he soon returned to royal favour, receiving numerous offices and titles.

The career of his son, Charles II d'Amboise, was brilliant but short. At twenty, he was Governor of Paris; when King Louis XII came to the throne, he was created *grand maître de la maison du roi*. Most of his time was spent leading the French armies in Italy. He was created both Marshal and Admiral of France and, as Governor of Milan, became a virtual Viceroy. The phrase '*Milan a fait Meillant*' is a tribute both to the splendour of his Château and his unhesitating use of the Italian revenues. In 1511, at the height of his fortune and power, he died, just as Meillant was nearing completion. Injured in a game of snowballs, it is said by a snowball containing a stone, he fell in full armour from his horse while

Preceding pages (left): *The magnificent main front of Meillant, with the two staircase towers: the Tour des Cerfs on the left and the Tour du Lion on the right.*
(right): *The* salon, *dominated by a massive fireplace incorporating a minstrels' gallery.*

Right: *The dining room is a sumptuous example of Gothic Revival, carried out for the duchesse de Mortemart during extensive restoration by the architect Louis Normand.*

crossing a bridge into a freezing river, catching a chill from which he rapidly died.

The magnificent main front of Meillant is dominated by two staircase towers, the Tour des Cerfs on the left, still wholly Gothic, and the Tour du Lion on the right, mixing Gothic and Renaissance detail. Here, the walls are emblazoned with interlaced Cs and with flaming mountains – *chauds monts* – for Chaumont on the Loire. Above is a tier carved with figures of soldiers looking through an arcade, a motif inspired by the figures of servants leaning out of blind windows in the famous Palais Jacques Coeur in Bourges. To the right, the Tour des Sarrassins is emblazoned with Ls and fleurs-de-lys, marking a visit by King Louis XII, complete with his emblem, a porcupine.

In 1552, the Château de Meillant passed from the Amboise family to Charles de La Rochefoucauld-Barbezieux, then in 1600 to the Brichanteau, in 1710 to the Gorge d'Antraigues and in 1732 to Paul François de Béthune, the great duc de Charost. The Duke was one of the few aristocrats remaining in France to escape the guillotine, and his survival was due to his enormous popularity in Berry. The Duke bequeathed his fortune to his second wife, who, in 1837, left Meillant to her niece Virginie de Sainte-Aldegonde.

Gothic Revival in France was pioneered more by artists than by architects, notably the artists of the Troubadour school, whose work dominated the Salon of 1817. The architect Benjamin Ferrey, in his *Recollections of Pugin*, describes a tour of Normandy in 1825: 'the grand monastic ruins and desecrated churches in France were not regarded with much reverence either by their custodians or by tourists … By bribing those in charge of these precious remains, persons were allowed to detach and carry away any ornamental fragment they desired …'

In 1838, the novelist Prosper Mérimée, then newly appointed Inspector of Historical Monuments, noted of Meillant in his *Voyage d'Auvergne* that 'all the apartments have been altered on several occasions, and there is not one where the furnishing or the decoration dates from before the 18th century. Only the fireplaces, as large as a modern room, appear to date from the original construction: all are of an excessive simplicity.' According to Mérimée, the duc de Mortemart had already embarked on repairs and work was largely finished by 1850, when an article appeared in the *Magasin Pittoresque*. His architect was Louis Normand, who,

inspired by Pugin in England, set out to show that medieval interiors had been full of strong vivid colour.

The original broad spiral stone staircases survived in both towers rising to rich ribbed vaults. The main entrance in the Tour des Cerfs leads into the Salle des Cerfs, which takes its name from three large wooden stags mounted with real antlers, the best way to display them before taxidermy was perfected. Immediately above is the *salon*, dominated by a massive two-tier fireplace incorporating a minstrels' gallery above the hearth. This is painted with scenes of the Château's history, very much in the Troubadour vein. One represents the so-called *table des trois seigneurs* where in ancient times the lords of Meillant and two neighbouring fiefs were said to have met in the woods to parley in the open air. The walls, panelled to shoulder height, incorporate some original Flamboyant carving; the ceiling beams are brightly painted with blue-and-white arabesques and rest on a rich, gilded Gothic cornice.

Normand's work is seen at its most complete in the dining room, lined with richly coloured 'Spanish' leather pressed into elaborate patterns. The room is dominated by a massive chimneypiece emblazoned with interlaced Cs and *chauds monts*. The stonework is picked out in green and red with touches of gold as well as bands of geometric patterning. The richly ribbed ceiling, adorned with numerous pendants, is also picked out in gold with inset panels painted with elaborate patterns of enamel-like brilliance.

Against the walls stand handsome Gothic Revival dressers with linenfold panels and shelves for displaying pewter and porcelain. Contemporary ornamental glass survives in the windows glazed in interlocking octagons.

The duc de Mortemart died in 1875, but Meillant still belongs to his descendants and is one of a series of grand châteaux on the Route Jacques Coeur which are open most of the year. Reflected in the still waters of its moats, with green grass lapping at the walls, Meillant is today far from a fortress, for all its numerous towers; instead, it offers a reminder of the extraordinary splendour of the late Middle Ages.

Above: *The plainer exterior of the Château, looking over the moat.*

Right: *Details of Flamboyant Gothic and Renaissance carving, including* (top left) *the flaming mountains (*chauds monts*) which were the arms of the Amboise family.*

EIGHTEEN

HÔTEL DE LAUZUN

PARIS

The Hôtel de Lauzun represents the high-water mark of a style that has rarely been equalled before or since for intensity of ornament and colour – the restless, gilded, highly wrought *style* Mazarin.

Charles Gruyn des Bordes bought the site, now 17 Quai d'Anjou, in 1641, although the house was not built until 1656–61.

Gruyn was one of a group of financiers who amassed enormous fortunes in the 1640s and 1650s, taking advantage of Mazarin's lack of concern with the methods they used to raise money for him. In 1655, Gruyn obtained the coveted post of commissar-general to the light cavalry, bringing him numerous military victualling contracts, and the following year he became one of the select group who managed the *gabelle*, the salt tax which then provided about a fifth of the annual revenue of the State.

He evidently realised that his position was far from secure, for the marriage contract made with his second wife, Geneviève de Mouy, in 1657 specifies that his new house should be in her name.

129

She was a marquise, and he made full show of this, linking his arms – three boars' heads – with hers on all the firebacks, and repeating their interlaced initials, M and G, in every part of the house. Hardly was the house complete when Gruyn was arrested by Colbert and quickly condemned.

After his death, in around 1680, his children sold the house in 1682 to Antonin Nompar, comte de Lauzun, famous in history as the fiancé, and perhaps the husband, of La Grande Mademoiselle, the daughter of Gaston d'Orléans, Louis XIII's brother. Although he lived here for only three years, it is from him that the house takes its name. After changing hands many times, the house was bought in 1928 by the City of Paris to avert a threat that the interiors would be dismantled and shipped to America.

The architect of the Hôtel de Lauzun was Charles Chamois, who worked for the famous marquis de Louvois. The principal apartment is on the second floor and consists of four stunningly ornate rooms that form an enfilade along the river front. Each doorcase has a richly modelled architrave, first laurel leaves, then oak and laurel leaves intermingled, and finally a boldly sculpted egg and dart moulding.

The Salon de Musique is panelled to its full height. Every surface, every moulding is painted or gilded as if to ensure that no one shall ever be able to alter the effect by so much as hanging a picture. Yet it is by no means untouched. The large mirrors are encased in delicately modelled frames that are clearly early-eighteenth-century, while the awkwardly cramped balconies were improvised soon after 1906.

The overwhelming effect of so much gilding is countered by the painted decoration, either applied over it or beside it, like the blue-and-yellow star pattern. The crowning magnificence of this room is its frescoed ceiling. Coved ceilings, unbroken by beams, were an innovation at this time, and the style of painting adopted here was based closely on Italy.

At the end of the enfilade is the most delightful room in the house, a small *cabinet* lined with mirrors, where the quality and invention of Gruyn's painters can be appreciated to the full. The ceiling is a golden sky of floating garlands held aloft by *putti*. Even at the time, there were some to whom such richness was unpalatable – La Fontaine said of the Château de Richelieu that 'there is so much gold that it annoys me' – but today the interiors have a deep burnished lustre and more subtle shades and tints of gold than can be counted.

Preceding pages (left): *Four stunningly ornate rooms form the enfilade. The Hôtel was built for the financier Charles Gruyn des Bordes in the late 1650s. Its magnificent interiors provide one of the finest examples of the* style Mazarin *at its most opulent.*
(right): *The frescoed ceiling of the* cabinet *creates an al fresco effect against a lustrous golden sky.*

Right: *The Salon de Musique. Every element of the decoration is as richly wrought as the most elaborate picture frame, with painted panels in the dado and a frieze sculpted with ivory-white* amorini.

NINETEEN

BAGATELLE

PICARDY

One of the most attractive traits of the eighteenth century was the attention it lavished on small buildings – garden temples and follies, belvederes, orangeries and *cottages ornées*. Few were so intricate as the *pavillons* and *maisons de rendez-vous* erected by French courtiers for their mistresses and liaisons. A refuge from the grandeur of Court life, they were intended for pleasure and retirement, for conversation, cards, picnics and supper parties – for surrendering to temptations of every kind. Their essence is different from the English villa or the German *Lustschloss*, both of which tended to be built for more prolonged retreat – for summer holidays rather than summer afternoons. These pavilions are found in large numbers around Paris and also around provincial towns; one of the most complete is Bagatelle, at Abbeville, once beyond the city walls and even now secluded amid lawns and trees.

Bagatelle, appropriately enough, means a trifle, and according to the poet Sedaine, writing soon after the house was completed, it was the owner, Abraham Van Robais, who gave it the name. Van Robais was a leading textile manufacturer who Voltaire described as '*menait train de Prince*'. Abraham was the grandson of José Van Robais, who had been induced by Colbert, Louis XIV's great minister, to settle at Abbeville in 1665 and establish a textile works, bringing in both workmen and equipment from his factory in Middelburg, in Holland. Colbert's main objectives were for France to gain ascendancy in the textile trade and to put a check on rapidly increasing imports from England and Holland. Among the inducements he offered to Van Robais were a gift of 12,000 livres, an interest-free loan of 40,000 livres, a monopoly within 10 leagues of Abbeville, and the right for him and his workmen to practise their religion as Calvinists – though not to build a church.

Colbert's correspondence shows that his agents made assiduous attempts to convert them before the infamous revocation of the Edict of Nantes in 1685, which led to the slaughter of thousands of Protestants. These efforts were in vain and in the event their freedom of worship was never withdrawn – an extraordinary tribute to the importance attached by the French Crown to the factory. The privileges were renewed on successive occasions until, in 1784, it was raised to the status of a *manufacture royale*.

The size of the Van Robais establishment was constantly remarked on by travellers. In his *Travels in France* (1789), Arthur Young observed that 'the buildings are very large ... They say 1500 hands are employed of which 250 are weavers ... Beside fine cloths they make at Abbeville carpets, tapestry, worsted stockings, barracans (a light cloth worn by the clergy), minorques and ... cotton handkerchiefs.'

The deeds show that Abraham Van Robais acquired the site for Bagatelle on 30 August 1751 and made further purchases of adjacent land on 28 January 1753 and 5 January 1754. The latter mentions a '*pavillon et jardin*' already complete, implying the house was built in 1751–54. Miraculously, the house has escaped intact the successive wars that have engulfed Picardy.

In 1787, Van Robais sold Bagatelle to his brother André, who resold it '*tout meublé*' to Pierre-Firmin Roze. In 1795, it was bought by Charles-Joseph Mathurel, who is thought to have sold off some of the furniture. Three years later, it passed to Nicolas-François Cospin, who sold it in 1810 to Gabriel de Wailly.

Remarkably, no further changes were made to the house until shortly before the First World War, when two wings were added by the architect Parent, containing those Edwardian 'musts': a *salon de musique* and a billiard room. These were illustrated soon afterwards in *La Vie à la Campagne*, a French counterpart of *Country Life*, which was a victim of the Depression.

During the First World War, the newly created parterres had been turned over to vegetables. In 1918, three bombs fell in the garden, fortunately doing no damage to the house. In 1940, Bagatelle escaped the fearsome German bombardment of Abbeville, which destroyed two thousand houses, and the following year house and contents were put under military protection as a *Kunstdenkmal* by a proclamation of General von Stülpnagel.

M. Jacques de Wailly, writing for the Abbeville Société d'Emulation in 1943, put forward the idea that the house was built in three stages, beginning as a single-storey pavilion crowned by a balustrade. To this, he suggested the attic storey was added in around 1763, while the mansard roof was later still, possibly not until 1787. The thought came to him when floors were taken up over the dining room and Salon d'Hiver, revealing rafters sawn off in a telltale way. Certainly the external treatment of the *œil-de-bœuf* windows is decidedly Neo-Classical, with carved drapery of the kind that came into fashion in the 1760s. The evenness of the brickwork throughout suggests the whole house may have been re-cased at the same time. The drapery, of course, is a neat touch for a cloth manufacturer, akin to the *armes parlantes* of a soldier.

Inside, the staircase is ingeniously contrived within a small vestibule, with twin flights rising in perfect symmetry around a kidney-shaped well and meeting at a central landing. The stair is of oak and the panelling painted in four shades of green, the darker

Preceding pages (left): *The entrance front. This delightful pavilion on the edge of Abbeville was built for Abraham Van Robais, whose family had been enticed by Colbert from Holland in 1665 to set up a textile manufactory.*
(right): *The garden front, showing the wings added early in the twentieth century. Avenues of pleached limes surround an arena of lawn punctuated by cones of neatly clipped box.*

Above: *The staircase in the entrance hall. Twin flights are brilliantly contrived in a very small space.*

Right: *A view out through one of the œil-de-bœuf windows – typical French casement windows with matching glazing patterns.*

shades being used to pick out the edges of the panels. The lightest of touches is provided by the delicate wrought-iron rococo stair-rail, a perfect counterpoint of balancing S and C curves.

Double doors open into the circular Salon d'Été, which appropriately to its name is without a fireplace. Here, the superb rococo panelling writhes in energetic curves, bursting out to fill every blank piece of wall. Even the relatively sober arches over the doors are engulfed by surging mouldings.

The paintings of smoking urns and splashing fountains, surrounded by arabesques of trailing flowers, contain echoes of the boudoir of Marie Antoinette at Fontainebleau and were clearly added later, probably in the 1780s. The painted overdoors of *Morning, Midday* and *Evening* have been attributed to J. B. Huet, who was working at the nearby Château de Long. Although the original furniture, listed in an inventory taken in the Revolution *An* VI (1798), has disappeared, the cabriolet chairs have tops which

marry neatly with the bottoms of the panels behind. Another detail worth noting is the telescoping of the door reveals into the adjoining Salon d'Hiver, so steep that there are double doors on one side and a single one on the other. The Salon d'Hiver has more pretty rococo boiseries breaking forward over the fireplace and inset with tall mirrors. With the tall casement windows and the low dado, they give a sense of height to a low room.

Upstairs, the bedrooms are on an engagingly miniature scale, opening off an attractive D-shaped ante-room looking over the garden, with an elaborate parquet floor and pretty toile curtains. The bedrooms on either side are each equipped with a *cabinet* and *garderobe*, a doll's-house evocation of the matching apartments in great châteaux and palaces.

Today, Bagatelle belongs to new owners but remains a rare example of a small house that is open to the public and retains a lived-in feel.

Above: *Looking across the first-floor ante-room, with its unusual œil-de-bœuf window, to one of the bedrooms.*

Left (above): *The Salon d'Hiver, picked out in different shades of blue with a sky painted on the ceiling;* (below): *The Salon d'Été. The rococo panelling was painted with delicate Neo-Classical motifs, probably in the 1780s.*

TWENTY

VILLA KERYLOS

CÔTE D'AZUR

A friend once exclaimed to the painter Alma-Tadema: 'We all dream that we dwell in marble halls when your name is mentioned.'
But for Théodore Reinach, the mesmerising vision of antiquity conjured up by artists such as Alma-Tadema – of white marble,
splashing fountains, blue sea and brightly coloured interiors – did not remain a mere figment of the imagination.
At the Villa Kerylos, he built a house in which Ancient Greece takes on three-dimensional form. Every detail is modelled on
antique precedent, but the result is highly inventive and imaginative – a Grecian version of Art Nouveau in which the house becomes
a total work of art. Playing Greek may have been taken to extremes, but an evening with the Reinachs must have been
memorable and highly enjoyable.

Théodore Reinach was the youngest of three successful brothers. Their uncle, Jacques, Baron de Reinach, was born in Frankfurt but settled in Paris. Joseph, the eldest brother, wrote a prodigious seven-volume *Histoire de l'affaire Dreyfus*. Salamon was an archaeologist and philologue like his younger brother. Théodore was a child prodigy. René Cagnat, in a sketch of Reinach's life published in 1931, relates how aged thirteen, Théodore astonished a Russian lady by reciting the names of 130 Russian rivers. At the Lycée, he won nineteen prizes. 'Never,' said Cagnat, 'had such an accumulation of crowns been seen on a single head.' By the time his studies were complete, Reinach was an ardent Hellenist. His interest centred first on the coins of Asia Minor, and he was soon publishing at a furious rate, his researches ranging across chronology, epigraphy, mythology, art history and metrology, the science of weights and measures. In 1892, he turned to archaeology and was involved in excavations at Delphi.

Not surprisingly, the architect he chose to build his house, Emmanuel Pontremoli (1865–1956), was equally steeped in Greek studies. He had won the coveted Prix de Rome and had been to Pergamum and drawn a remarkable reconstruction of the site. In Paris, he had been appointed assistant architect at the Louvre, where he participated in the reconstruction of the Rubens Galleries and met Reinach.

The Villa Kerylos was named after a species of sea swallow whose name could be rendered equally well in Greek and French. Pontremoli's 1934 guide describes his idea of a house 'without date, appearing as if it had always been there'. Later, he wrote in his autobiographical memoir *Propos d'un solitaire* (1959): 'Reinach, occupied in his scientific work and his office as deputy, left me a completely free hand. I designed the furniture, the silver, the china. I had the hangings woven, even the linen. I designed the light fittings, the lamps.'

Great care was taken to preserve the trees on the point so that the villa did not look too bare; it is seen at its best from the promenade along the west shore of Cap Ferrat, where it stands out against the magnificent backdrop of mountains whose sheer cliffs have resisted development.

Pontremoli had a vision of a Mediterranean culture stronger than any specifically Greek or French traits. 'The Mediterranean house,' he wrote, 'has always developed around a peristyle, whatever the name it has been given: aulé, atrium, patio, even cloister.' Kerylos is designed around a peristyle, modelled, he said, on the houses of Delos.

Preceding pages (left): The Naiades, *or plunge bath, supplied with both hot and cold running water. The Villa Kerylos, a lavish recreation of an Ancient Greek villa, was built in 1902–07 for the archaeologist Théodore Reinach, to the designs of Emmanuel Pontremoli.*
(right): The Villa Kerylos, seen from Cap Ferrat. It stands on a terrace built on a rocky point with Beaulieu-sur-Mer behind.

Right: The Atrium. Columns, entablature and paving are all in polished white Carrara marble.

All the rooms in the house were given Greek names. In the entrance, or *Thyrôreion*, all is shade, providing relief from the heat outside. In the peristyle, the marble columns are all monoliths, single shafts of stone, chosen in the Carrara quarries by the mason Nicoli. During a short sharp shower, the lions' heads in the cornice spout water into the courtyard till the paving is awash, producing brilliant reflections as the sun emerges. A note of colour is introduced by the acroteria fronting the ridges of the roof tiles. These are executed in red and black, modelled on ones found on the Acropolis at Athens.

The *Andron*, or *grand salon*, runs along the south side of the peristyle. The walls are faced in coloured marbles chosen and arranged according to their figuring so that, for example, the grain in the narrow panels on either side of the doors is neatly balanced without being exactly matching. The mosaic floor is patterned like a large carpet, complete with fringe. At the west end is an altar to an unknown deity.

The *Triklinos*, or *salle à trois lits*, served as a dining room. The tables are set at right angles to each other with the fourth side left open for servants to approach. Reinach presided in the ancient manner, reclining on a couch.

Reinach's library was on the east front, to catch the morning light. This followed Vitruvius, who advised that libraries should look east to avoid exposing manuscripts to the humid winds from the south and south-west. The names of Greek writers are inscribed on the walls. Both furniture and cupboards are made of oak, inlaid and pegged with ivory. Among the chairs are two on a swan pattern, modelled on an Egyptian chair in the Louvre. Reinach stood up to write, following Greek custom.

Above: *The walls of the* Andron, *or* grand salon, *are faced in marble, with a stencil-painted frieze and wooden ceiling picked out in bright colours.*

Left: *Looking towards the house altar in the* Andron. *The original Grecian furniture and carefully concealed electric-light fittings survive.*

Mindful that cleanliness was central to Ancient Greek life, the Reinachs had elaborate provision for bathing. Immediately inside the entrance is the *Naiades*, a large plunge bath which brings to mind Alma-Tadema's painting of 1909, *A Favourite Custom*, portraying naked ladies bathing in an indoor pool.

On the first floor, the Reinachs had a suite of five rooms overlooking the sea, with a bedroom at either end, an adjoining bathroom and a central sitting room, the *Triptoleme*. All traces of twentieth-century plumbing were carefully hidden. The lavatories were shut away in cubicles; the baths were on the model of sarcophagi, carved from solid marble with running water. For wash basins, Pontremoli provided bronze tripod stands supporting silvered bronze bowls. The bidets, all-important in France, provided a particular challenge. They were concealed in chests – a door opens and they pull out on runners. Madame Reinach had a handsome porcelain bowl fully plumbed, her husband a lightweight metal version without running water. As mirrors were unknown in Ancient Greece, Pontremoli provided near-full-length looking glasses concealed behind folding panels in the doors.

Madame Reinach's bedroom, Les Oiseaux, is blue, in contrast to the Pompeiian red of her husband's. She had a double bed, while he had a single, set behind fluted columns and screened by curtains. Hers had hangings made by Ecochard. The light tones contrast with the deep resonant blues of the recesses behind the columns.

The house was illuminated throughout by electric light, cleverly concealed within specially designed fittings. The chandeliers are double circles of lights, inspired, said Pontremoli, by the characteristic hanging lamps in mosques, permissible here as a *reflet byzantin*. While most early electric-light fittings left the bulb exposed, at Kerylos every light has shades, usually of alabaster, the type known as a cocked-hat light. In addition, there are standard lamps – lights set on tall, thin three-legged stands that in antiquity carried oil lamps. Wall brackets and table lamps also survive.

Right: *The enfilade, seen from Reinach's bathroom. Each room has a mosaic floor on a different pattern.*

Below: *The* Triklinos, *or dining room, where Théodore Reinach ate reclining on the raised daybed.*

Reinach, for all his archaeological interests and the opportunities for acquisition that must have come with them, eschewed the display of antique pieces, preferring to have pieces made specially or simply to buy reproductions of *objets d'art* from museums. 'We bought,' wrote Pontremoli in his autobiography, 'bronzes in Naples, utensils copied from Herculaneum and Pompei which could easily find place in his Mediterranean house.' Much of the furniture was designed by Pontremoli and made by Bettenfeld. Almost all the wooden furniture – tables, chairs and footstools – bears the stamp of both men.

On his death, Reinach left the house, complete with all its contents, to the Institut de France. Their foresight in accepting such a recent creation is as important as his generosity. His papers, alas, appear to have been destroyed in Paris during the War, but the house remains in excellent condition and is open to the public throughout the year. In summer concerts and operas are held in the atrium, which thanks to the abundance of marble is held by musicians to have a fantastic acoustic, even though they are performing in the open air.

Top: *Reinach's Pompeiian red bedroom. The palmette pattern behind the bed was inspired by decoration on terracotta sarcophagi.*

Above: *Madame Reinach's bedroom.*

Left: *The library was as much a total work of art as contemporary Art Nouveau houses.*

TWENTY-ONE

CASA DE PILATOS

SEVILLE

As the reconquest of southern Spain proceeded, the Spanish took to the Moorish way of life – of cool green courtyards
and shaded loggias, so well suited to the heat of Andalusían summers. This feature of Sevillian houses may have still older origins:
the layout of houses in the great city of Itálica, birthplace of the Emperors Hadrian and Trajan, a few miles away, has striking similarities.
Such Classical parallels were probably present in the minds of the younger members of noble families, more travelled and
better educated than their bellicose fathers who fought until the last Moorish stronghold in Granada fell in 1492. Among this younger
generation, Don Fadrique Enríquez de Ribera, 1st Marquis of Tarifa, occupies a place of central importance.

After a pilgrimage to the Holy Land and a stay in Italy, between 1518 and 1520, Don Fadrique returned to Seville to renovate a palace begun by his parents.

He instituted the pious devotion of the Way of the Cross. Starting as it did with 'Christ shown to the people in the praetorium of Pilate', this soon led to the popular belief that the palace was fashioned after Pilate's house in Jerusalem, the plans of which Don Fadrique had brought from the Holy Land, giving birth to the unusual name Casa de Pilatos.

The house, substantially complete at the time of Don Fadrique's death in 1539, successfully combines three different styles and traditions: late Gothic vaulting and decoration in the Flemish manner of Seville Cathedral, as seen in the chapel; plaster decoration and polychrome tiles in the Moorish style which was still practised by local craftsmen; and finally Classical marble columns, statues and fountains imported from Italy and used in the gardens and loggias. To this, the descendants of the Marquis, the 1st and 3rd Dukes of Alcalá, who were both Spanish Viceroys in Naples,

Preceding pages (left): *A sixteenth-century wrought-iron grille with cherubs and chimeras flanking the Enríquez coat of arms.*
(right): *The Patio Grande or central courtyard.*

Above: *Looking over the entrance courtyard to the Patio Grande.*

Right: *In the upper arcade of the Patio Grande, a series of wall paintings of literary worthies, set within* trompe l'œil *arcades, has been revealed; these date from 1539. The geometric ornament above the arches is still Moorish in character.*

added elements in a much purer Italian vein, filling it with a famous collection of antique sculpture.

The family's rise was closely allied with the dawning of the new golden age in Spanish history. In the fifteenth century, Seville had been torn by the bloody strife between two great feudal families, the Ponces de León, Dukes of Arcos, and the Guzmanés, Dukes of Medina Sidonia. By the opening years of the sixteenth century, however, the ruthless policies of King Fernando and Queen Isabella had re-established peace in the city with the support of a new aristocracy which had prospered through trade with the New World. Don Pedro Enríquez, the father of Don Fadrique, was said to share with his nephew, King Fernando, a measure of Jewish blood. Don Pedro was a highly successful businessman with ventures both in trade with the Indies and in the manufacture of soap in a factory on the banks of the Guadalquivir River on which Seville stands.

Above: Panels of geometric tiles surmounted by honeycomb decoration have a Moorish feel, illustrating how the Spaniards fell in love with the cool patios they discovered after the Reconquista in 1492.

Left: The lower arcades of the Patio Grande are faced with tiles designed in the manner of carpets.

For all his alleged Jewish ancestry, Don Pedro was a zealous Christian and firm supporter of the Inquisition. He married successively two sisters, Doña Beatriz and Doña Catalina (mother of Don Fadrique), who brought to the marriage the riches of the Ribera family.

In 1483, Don Pedro and Doña Catalina acquired a small mansion facing on to the Calle Imperial, which today runs along the back of the Casa de Pilatos. The cramped site was on the northern edge of the old quarter known as Barrio de Santa Cruz, the former Jewish ghetto, and a considerable distance from the Alcázar and the Cathedral. But it had an important advantage: a steady supply of water from the Aqueduct of the Caños de Carmona, just outside the city walls.

The Marquis kept a diary of his progress through Italy. In Florence he was a guest of the Medici, while he was in Rome for the magnificent obsequies on the death of Raphael. His greatest enthusiasm was for the Certosa de Pavía, of which he wrote 'it is the best house that can be imagined … all built of marble most minutely worked'. Upon his return from Palestine, he visited the workshops of two of the leading Genoese sculptors who had worked in the Certosa and ordered the splendid monuments to his father and mother, which can now be seen back in their original position in the chapterhouse of the Monastery of Santa María de las Cuevas.

Though the columns in the Patio Grande are Classical in proportions, the arches they carry, some flattened, some stilted, with the heavy mouldings and stucco decoration, still have an earlier feel. A more Roman note was introduced by the 1st Duke of Alcalá, with four giant statues in the corners and a series of Emperors' busts in niches around the lower arcade.

The Emperors and other Roman worthies were restored for the Viceroy by a sculptor named Giuliano Menichini who added the bust of Charles V to those of Roman Emperors. To strengthen the idea of the house as Pilate's Praetorium, the Duke obtained from Pope Pius V a replica of the marble column at the Vatican, against which Christ was said to have been scourged, placing it at the entrance to his chapel. It may also have been the Duke who gave the rooms around the courtyard their fancy names: the Salón del Pretorio, the Gabinete de Pilatos and the Descanso de los Jueces (retiring room of the judges). These cool tiled rooms were used in the summer, while the winter apartments were above, hung with tapestry. The tiles, or *azulejos*, are designed to look like textile hangings, with the arms of Enríquez and Ribera alternating at the centre of each.

The most elaborate arrangement of tiles is on the staircase. Above, the plasterwork and honeycomb-pattern gilt wooden dome are still Moorish in style. The dome, dated 1538, is the work of Cristóbal Sánchez, member of the famous dynasty of master carpenters active in Seville in the early sixteenth century. In the upper arcade of the Patio Grande, the walls are frescoed with portraits of Classical writers set within *trompe l'œil* arcades. These have only recently been uncovered beneath multiple coats of whitewash and have been dated in 1539.

The Marquis had only two daughters, both born out of wedlock, his early marriage having been annulled without issue. So, on his death, the Casa de Pilatos was inherited by his nephew, who in 1558 was created Duke of Alcalá. He added the Jardín Grande, a vast new patio to the south-east. His architect was an Italian, Benvenuto Tortelli, whom he sent from Naples in 1568. Tortelli's new courtyard is in a much purer and more correct Classical style, with a Doric order below and a Corinthian above. Work was brought to a halt by the premature death of the Viceroy in Naples in 1571. An inventory drawn up later nonetheless conveys the

riches of the magnificent collection of antique and Renaissance sculpture, medals and cameos he had amassed while in Italy.

Like his uncle, the Duke died without a direct male heir, so the title went to a nephew, whose son, the 3rd Duke, largely completed the construction of the house as it stands today. The special license which he was granted gives an idea of the vast household he supported, with a private printing press, a permanent roster of musicians and an astrologer, while in his palace he entertained a circle of painters, sculptors, poets and philosophers.

After the house passed to the Dukes of Medinaceli in the middle of the seventeenth century, as a result of the 7th Duke's marriage to the heiress of the Enríquez de Ribera family, it was occupied by agents and tenants. Parts of the buildings suffered the ravages of the French occupation in 1808 and were bombed during the civil disorders of 1843. Richard Ford, in his famous *Handbook for Travellers in Spain*, published in 1845, despairs of the state of the property: 'All is now in a scandalous state of neglect. The saloons of state are whitewashed and turned to base purposes, the gardens are running wild, the sculpture is tossed about as in a mason's yard.' As the owners of vast states elsewhere in Spain, the family hardly visited Seville; the situation only began to change in the second half of the nineteenth century, but even then they made few alterations to the structure of the house.

In the late 1850s, the family once again took up occasional residence in Seville, and tactful restorations begun – the most regrettable change being the paving in the Patio Grande in marble in place of the original Moorish brick tile.

The Casa de Pilatos is now vested in the Medinaceli Foundation, which cares for nearly eighty historic family properties. It is run by the Duchess's youngest son, the Duke of Segorbe, Seville and Spain's most energetic preservationist. Once again artisans and craftsmen have workshops in the house, not only working in the Casa de Pilatos itself but in a whole series of properties across the city.

Above: *The Renaissance loggia built in the late 1560s to the designs of the Neapolitan architect Benvenuto Tortelli.*

Right: *The coach house, originally intended by the Duke of Alcalá as a new entrance to the house.*

PALACIO DE OCA

GALICIA

Some of the most beautiful and romantic houses in Europe are those which appear to grow from the landscape. The *pazos*, or manors, of Galicia are built of the local stone to an almost timeless pattern, with a strong four-square tower invariably proclaiming the ancestry of the place. This is an architecture that has always looked back as much as forward and as a result has an individuality and power of its own. Thanks to prodigious rainfall brought by the Atlantic westerlies, the region is green and lush, and in the sun the grey granite is given a golden hue by lichens that thrive in the clean air.

The estate at Oca, which at one time consisted of about 10,000 hectares, was one of the largest in Galicia and has a record of almost unbroken habitation since the twelfth century. The enormously thick walls of the tower may incorporate masonry of this date, though it was probably raised to its present height by Don Suero de Oca in the early fifteenth century.

Despite these defences, Suero de Oca's sworn enemy, the powerful Archbishop of Santiago, took advantage of one of his absences in 1447 to abduct his wife and sequestrate his property. It was not until 1564 that Pope Pius V conceded the estate to King Philip II, who sold it to Doña Maria de Neira, a patrician lady of Santiago. Claiming to be one of the oldest families in Galicia, the de Neiras were said to descend from the mythical Reina Loba, the wolf queen who slew a serpent on the banks of the River Neyra, whence they derived their name and crest.

Oca has passed by inheritance ever since, and the bewildering changes of name of its owners are explained by the Spanish system of primogeniture which allows a daughter to inherit if there is no surviving son. The house was remodelled in the early eighteenth

Top: *The east front, seen from the terrace leading to the chapel. The* cour d'honneur *below also serves as the village square.*

Above: *The chapel of San Antonio.*

Right: *Looking down into the chapel from the family gallery. The reredos is dated 1750.*

shapes. The characteristic Galician *merlons*, or battlements, here have the rough-hewn points of ancient menhirs. Usually it is the topiary that provides the accents in a formal garden; here it is the standing stones, which line the sloping sides of the two basins, alternately spherical and pointed. At the top of the upper pond, where the mill stands, the spheres are impaled on the shortened, stubby obelisks, while the lower cross walks are adorned with urns, some of stone, others more exotically of blue-and-white porcelain.

This water garden is an allegory: the upper pond (the *Estanque de Arriba*) represents heaven and contains a stone boat with statues of the master and his servant (reinstated since these photographs were taken), while the lower pond (the *Estanque de Abajo*) represents hell, with a serpent's mouth gushing water and creating turbulence. Here, the boat retains its cannons and solemn figures on the prow and stern.

The ponds were probably created between 1715 and 1720, when Andres Gayoso and his wife, Constanza Arias Ozores, began remodelling the house. Esteban Ferreiro, a well-known sculptor from Santiago, signed a contract in October 1717 to carve the stone figure of a giant with a serpent (the crest of the de Neiras), to be completed by 1720.

Today, Oca, like Pilatos, is immaculately maintained by the Duke of Segorbe, who runs the Medinaceli Foundation set up by his mother. As abundant water rushes past you down a dozen rills and channels, threading its way under the pyramid-roofed laundry, there is an overwhelming feeling that the genius of the place has not merely been consulted by generations of owners but lives on in the greatest contentment.

century by Andres Gayoso de Neira and his wife, who introduced the central arched portal, flanked by rusticated columns and wide enough to admit coaches and farm carts. The ground floor, as usual in the Galician *pazo*, was devoted entirely to the production of the estate, with great grain chests, store rooms for drying flax, herbs and nuts, a bakery, a weaving room, and a *bodega* for the wine, equipped with vats and massive oak casks made by the village carpenters. The windows here are typically Galician, with simple lattices below and open grilles above.

All the principal family and guest rooms were on the first floor, with the kitchen and servery in an uncompleted wing at the end. Beside the unfinished masonry, there is a carved pointing finger bearing the inscription '*Prosiga*' (follow on) and the date 1746. Instead, Andres Gayoso's son Fernando decided to extend the house in the opposite direction, with a handsome Baroque chapel overlooking the little square in front of the house. It was designed by José Gambiño, one of the leading sculptors in Santiago. The elaborate twin towers oversailing the plain façade below provide an exotic silhouette, picked up by the finials, which sit on the balustrades at the sides like so many giant candlesticks. These provide a terrace walk connecting the house to a family gallery at the north end of the chapel.

The most intriguing room at Oca is the Cámara Principal, or main guest room, with sleeping cubicles named after the four continents. The present marbled decoration dates from restoration in the 1930s. The *brasero* for burning charcoal in the centre of the floor is a reminder that only two rooms had fireplaces before the nineteenth century. The saloon also retains a pair of sleeping alcoves, one adapted as a tiny oratory.

Like certain gardens in Brittany in which walls and paving are all formed of the local granite, the garden at Oca has a special resonance and dignity. It is at once noble and primitive: noble in the grand lines of the layout; primitive because the granite is hard to work and the stone must be carved into strong and simple

Preceding pages: *The upper pond, where the vertical accents provided by vases, stone balls and balustrades have survived all the changes in gardening fashion over three centuries.*

Top: *The patio and west front. Once the hub of activity on the pazo, it would have been filled with tenants bringing their rent in kind – corn, grapes and other produce – while they watered their horses at the fountain.*

Above: *The covered wash house, fed by a fast-flowing stream.*

Right: *The stone boat in the lower pond, complete with cannons and figures of a* señor *and his valet at the prow and stern.*

TWENTY-THREE

QUINTA DA REGALEIRA

SINTRA

Sintra has long been as famous for its exotic architecture as for its stunning scenery. Visitors have gazed in awe – and amusement – at the exotic royal palace dominated by a pair of chimneys looking like Staffordshire pottery kilns. They have walked out to visit Montserrate, a heady blend of Moorish palace and Turkish *seraglio*, and climbed through the woods to see the grotesque nineteenth-century mountain-top palace of Ferdinand of Saxe-Coburg, the artist king-consort to Queen Maria II.

Most tantalising of all is the series of extravagant Manueline gates, loggias and balustrades on the road out of Sintra towards Montserrate. These mark the long and secretive wall of the Quinta da Regaleira. If you are on foot, the rough pavement changes to mosaic emblazoned with stars as the property begins, just as the sidewalks are paved in marble in front of the grandest New York skyscrapers.

Regaleira is the creation of Antonio Augusto de Carvalho Monteiro (1850–1920). Carvalho was born in Brazil, in Rio, but spent most of his life in Portugal where he acquired the soubriquet of Monteiro-*Milhões* – Monteiro-millions – thanks to his immense fortune. He was a passionate bibliophile and collector, making a virtual museum of the Palácio Quintela in Lisbon. His specialities were butterflies, shells, clocks and silver, on which he spent prodigious sums, but his interests spread across both the arts and sciences and for many years he was president of the Zoological Garden in Lisbon.

Monteiro's architect was the Italian stage designer Luigi Manini (1848–1936). Born in Brescia, he had studied at the Brera Academy and then acted as assistant to Carlo Ferrario, professor of stage design at La Scala. In April 1879, he had arrived at the Teatro de S. Carlos in Lisbon as stage designer, remaining in Portugal until 1913. During this time he turned his attention to architecture and made a speciality of reviving Manueline Gothic, the fantastic late-Gothic style that flourished in late-fifteenth- and early-sixteenth-century Portugal, characterised by barnacle-encrusted naturalistic ornament. Like other architects of the period, he sought not just correctness but also to outdo his models in sheer dizzying exuberance. His best-known work is the Palace Hotel at Buşaco, begun in 1888 to a design sparked by the fourteenth-century Tower of Belem in Lisbon. In Sintra, he also designed a garden house and interiors at the Palácio Biester and the Cottage Sassetti, as well as decoration at the Teatro de Funchal, the Winter Garden at the Teatro de S. João, and a series of Portuguese pavilions at international exhibitions. Among his opera sets were those for *Aida*, *Lohengrin*, *Otello*, *Mephistoles* and *Guarany*.

Working closely with Manini at Regaleira was the sculptor José da Fonseca (1884–1956). Born in Coimbra, he had settled in Sintra, where he remained until his death. He was one of a group of sculptors who worked at Buşaco, and it is at Regaleira that his real virtuosity emerges. Manini was evidently able to coax him to heights of finesse he never achieved elsewhere.

At Regaleira, variety is the essence of Manini's approach: each window is treated differently; balconies and balustrades rarely repeat. Carving grows richer as it ascends until virtually the entire wall surface is encrusted with ornament.

Monteiro acquired the Quinta in 1900; his initials, C.M., and the date 1910 are inscribed on a plaque overlooking the road. Most of the buildings were probably complete by 1913 when Manini returned to Italy, and certainly by 1917, when – in neutral Portugal – Regaleira featured in the review *A Arquitectura Portugese*.

Preceding pages (left): *The entrance porch. Renaissance motifs are mixed with Gothic, while naturalistic branches and foliage fill the arches.*
(right): *The entrance gates. The Quinta Regaleira and its gardens were created for the Brazilian millionaire Antonio Augusto de Carvalho Monteiro by the Italian stage designer Luigi Manini.*

Right: *The stable block, with its abundance of carved ornament rivalling that of the house.*

The entrance porch combines both Gothic and Classical detail, with a band of Renaissance vases and medallions and knotted foliage set within the arch. The bases on the colonettes are treated differently on each side; that on the left is carved with sequins. Manini's freedom of invention is best illustrated by the balcony on the garden front. Immediately beneath is a life-size statue of Monteiro's wife, surrounded by her three grandchildren. One holds a lamb, one a puppy, and the third a duck. Cooing doves sit contentedly on the shawl she holds in front of her. The sentiment might be excessive but for the concentration required to pick out the details amid the amazing tangle of knotted ropes mixed with artichokes.

Just across from the house is the chapel, again Neo-Manueline, but slenderer in proportions and more filigree in its ornaments, as if a more sober tone was appropriate here. The stable block is almost as richly treated as the house, with arcades and terraces, and a profusion of ropework and life-like heads of horses over the stall doors. On the upper terrace are two dogs, presumably favourites of Monteiro, carved over the door. While the house and stables are principally of limestone, the other buildings, both cottages and some of the garden follies, are of rough-hewn blocks of granite set in a random pattern, giving them the rustic look favoured in 1900 French villas.

The dining room is dominated by a massive hooded fireplace of the type common in French medieval châteaux. Manini and Fonseca use it for an astonishing display of richly undercut carving: a hunt scene with rearing horses carved virtually in three dimensions, surmounted by a statue of a young huntsman and two hounds. Over the doors are further sculpted figures of huntsmen, while in the corners of the vault the corbels are carved with ducks and pheasants set against a background of reeds and grass – in the manner that stuffed birds were set against naturalistic backdrops in glass cases. The doors are covered in red velvet and overlaid with Gothic brass hinges and borders, complete with the original lock cases and bolts. Originally, both walls and ceilings were frescoed; only two panels remain on either side of the fireplace – not, it has to be said, of the same quality as the carving. A mosaic floor, to a swirling pattern of leaves and branches, completes the treatment. Nearby, a drawing room has a very rich Portuguese Baroque ceiling constructed entirely of wood, with the timbers laid in a geometrical pattern, like a parquet floor, overlaid with richly carved shellwork, branches and leaves.

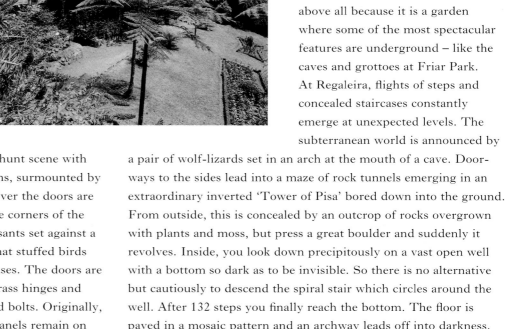

The excitement of Regaleira lies above all in its garden, which deserves comparison with Sir Frank Crisp's astounding garden at Friar Park, near Henley-on-Thames in England. The essence of the design – appropriately from Manini – lies in theatricality. It is conceived like a series of stage sets, with the emphasis on surprise. Whether surprise is a proper element for a garden was a subject for debate at the time. Sir Frank Crisp, in his abridged guide to Friar Park, quotes the warring parties. To Charles Thonger, author of the *Book of Garden Design* (1905), 'the making of surprises, such as the sudden revealing of unsuspected features in the garden scene, must always be considered as evidence of a debased taste, the prostituting of a beautiful art, for the sake of securing a momentary exclamation of astonishment on the part of an ignorant visitor.' R. Clinton Sturgis in *English Gardens* (1902) had taken the opposite view, writing that 'in the most interesting gardens the element of the unexpected is always present and the fact that it cannot be a surprise to the owner does not really detract from its value'.

Surprise at Regaleira comes partly from the views suddenly presented along winding drives and paths, but above all because it is a garden where some of the most spectacular features are underground – like the caves and grottoes at Friar Park. At Regaleira, flights of steps and concealed staircases constantly emerge at unexpected levels. The subterranean world is announced by a pair of wolf-lizards set in an arch at the mouth of a cave. Door-ways to the sides lead into a maze of rock tunnels emerging in an extraordinary inverted 'Tower of Pisa' bored down into the ground. From outside, this is concealed by an outcrop of rocks overgrown with plants and moss, but press a great boulder and suddenly it revolves. Inside, you look down precipitously on a vast open well with a bottom so dark as to be invisible. So there is no alternative but cautiously to descend the spiral stair which circles around the well. After 132 steps you finally reach the bottom. The floor is paved in a mosaic pattern and an archway leads off into darkness. Turn the first corner and a glimmer of daylight appears, and as your eyes become better accustomed to the dark, you can edge to

Above: *Looking towards the house from the chapel. The treatment of balustrades and windows, all carved with a profusion of ornament, changes from level to level.*

Right: *The inverted 'Tower of Pisa' descending vertically into the rock.*

the end of the tunnel, which appears behind an arch inset with reptilian figures suggestive of wolf-lizards.

This remarkable descent is undoubtedly inspired by a similar Renaissance stair shaft descending into the ground at Orvieto, in central Italy, designed by Antonio Sangallo the Younger. Further tunnels branch off deeper into the hillside, leading to a second well staircase, not quite so broad or deep but constructed in rough grotto style of blocks of weathered honeycombed limestone. This is encircled by three narrow galleries scarcely high enough to stand in, linked by a spiral stair at the side.

In these tunnels, part natural, part man-made, water for Sintra's gardens was sought. The natural stone is granite with a smooth surface. To make the caves more atmospheric, the walls and roof are encrusted with tufa, hanging like stalactites and forming pillars; calcium carbonate, a mild acid, was sometimes poured over them to produce this effect. Raul Proença's guidebook *Giua de Portugal* (*c*.1923) described these tunnels as '*luminadas a luz eletrica*'. The entire network, it seems, was originally lit by electric light, like the grotto of Venus at Linderhof, in Germany.

Top left: *Detail of the garden front, showing Monteiro's wife surrounded by her grandsons.*

Top right: *Carved wooden ceiling in Portuguese Baroque style.*

Above right: *Grappling wolf-lizards at the entrance to one of the tunnels.*

Left: *The dining room. A mosaic floor and brass door furniture complement Fonseca's virtuoso carving.*

TWENTY-FOUR

KASTEEL DE HAAR

UTRECHT

With its tall towers reflected in a broad moat, De Haar is a breathtaking vision of medieval pageantry and romance: a castle in the
full plumage of the age of chivalry, with a silhouette of steep roofs and lucarnes bristling with finials and wind vanes,
wooden wall walks hanging out over the towers, and scarlet-and-white chevron-painted shutters adding colour to walls of pale tawny brick.
De Haar is a re-creation to be compared with Cardiff Castle in Wales, Haut-Königsberg in Alsace, and Bousov, the castle of the
Teutonic knights in Moravia. It was undertaken by Baron Etienne van Zuylen van Nyevelt van de Haar,
whose family claimed descent from the Roman soldier Colonna, the alleged founder of the city of Utrecht. The Baron had been
brought up in Brussels. In 1887, he married Baroness Hélène de Rothschild and soon had acquired a house in the
Bois de Boulogne and another, Il Paradiso, in Nice.

When he began the restoration of De Haar, the Baron was in his thirties. All that remained was the much-decayed shell of the two principal wings and the stump of the great north-east tower. Probably begun in the thirteenth century, the castle had been rebuilt in the fourteenth century, largely pulled down following a siege of 1482, and rebuilt in the first half of the sixteenth century. The Baron and P. J. H. Cuypers, the leading architect in the Netherlands, decided to restore it to the state of 1530, romanticising the skyline but paying great attention to defensive detail.

Inspiration had come through the lawyer, historian and man of letters Victor de Stuers, who played a key role in establishing the

Preceding pages (left): Four years after his marriage to Hélène de Rothschild in 1887, Baron Etienne van Zuylen van Nyevelt van de Haar began restoring his ruined family castle with the architects P. J. H. and Joseph Cuypers. At the time, the great north-east tower was no more than a stump. (right): The park, seen beyond the roofs of the house from the tallest tower. The hall lies below the twisting hull-like roof on the right.

Left: Looking down on the hall, with its abundance of rich Gothic carving.

Below: Cuypers roofed over the old courtyard to form the hall, seen here from the gallery.

Dutch *Monumentenzorg* (office for the care of monuments). Soon after the Baron's marriage, Stuers had sent him drawings showing the state of De Haar with a draft restoration plan by the architect Adriaan Mulder. On 24 September 1890, de Stuers wrote to Cuypers, who had designed the splendid revivalist Central Station in Amsterdam and was still at work on the Rijksmuseum: 'Baron van Zuylen van Nyefelt van de Haar, married to a Rothschild in Paris [that says it all] … writes to me: "How much would it cost to restore the Château? Of course if I follow through with this project, I will construct the whole as *the most perfect ensemble*, and capable of giving us the most exact idea of what the château was in former days, that is to say I will not shrink from any sacrifice to achieve the summum of perfection, in other words to make a kind of living museum like Pierrefonds, but capable of being lived in for the month of August for example." '

Cuypers, amazingly, believed that the project could be completed in a year. The Baron thought two. Not surprisingly, work continued over twenty years, and the last drawings for the chapel were only made months before the First World War. The staple of Cuypers' practice was church building, and as a Catholic he had

benefited from the demand for new churches following the restoration of the Catholic Episcopal hierarchy in 1853. To supply stained glass and other furnishings and fittings, he established a studio for craftsmen at Roermond in the south of Holland where he lived. Cuypers' son, Joseph, in the big book published on the restoration of the castle wrote: 'a whole school of artists, formed under the management of a single master ... show us, that in working after the solid systems of the Middle Ages, one can obtain results that are similar, or even superior, to those of that glorious epoch.'

On 7 November 1891, the Baron wrote in excitement to his agent Lutyen: 'this restoration of my ruin of De Haar is ... feasible ... but it will cost an enormous amount of money'. To inaugurate the first completed room, the Baron arrived on 3 July 1893 with a number of friends for a lunch of salmon, beef, young turkey and lobster, and a pastry centrepiece of the new castle arising from the ruins. Plans for an additional guest wing, the *châtelet*, were drawn up the same year, with a *bel étage* containing two suites with saloons and marble-floored bathrooms. This is linked to the castle by a covered wooden bridge.

In rebuilding the castle, Cuypers carefully followed the lines of the old external walls, but roofed over the castle courtyard using steel girders to create the vast hall. As a result, the windows are at third-floor level, and filled with stained glass. The room is conceived as a hymn to the family's piety and ancestry. The north and east sides bear the statues of ten illustrious van Zuylens, van Nyevelts and van de Haars, including Etienne van Nyevelt, an early-sixteenth-century Grand Master of the Teutonic Order in Utrecht, and Dirk van Zuylen van de Haar and his wife, Josina, under whom the house achieved its apogee in the mid-sixteenth century. The stained glass at the top shows the Presentation of the Grand Charter of Utrecht by Arnolde van Hoorne, the 50th Prince-Bishop, in 1375. To uphold the Charter, the league of the Nyevelts was formed against Prince-Bishop David of Burgundy, and it was in the ensuing conflict that De Haar was burnt.

The corbels supporting the first-floor gallery represent the four states of society – labourer, bourgeois, soldier and scholar. The second tier symbolises earth, water and air. The roundels on the second-floor gallery portray the Madonna and child, St Etienne, the Baron's patron saint, and St George, the patron saint of chivalry. On another side, the figures on the balcony by Nieuwendijk are musicians being conducted from a corner by a statue of Cuypers himself. Below, the corbels are carved with figures in a tournament – trumpeters, esquires, herald and jester.

For so large a castle there are surprisingly few reception rooms, reflecting the limited space within the shell. The *Ridderzaal*, or Knights' Hall, is hung with dark-green velvet (*velours d'Utrecht*) embroidered with van Zuylen columns and van De Haar diamonds in gold. The magnificent chandelier of galloping horsemen is based

Left: *The ballroom, or salle des fêtes; the Baron's portrait hangs at the end.*

on a medieval example illustrated by Viollet-le-Duc. In the *salle des fêtes*, troubadours replace tournaments. At one end is a Gothic fireplace as elaborate as a cathedral high altar, with an extraordinary high-relief scene of the castle of love beside it, in which knights who scale the battlements are rewarded with crowns by maidens within. The panels forming a frieze at the other end of the room, inspired by Lucca della Robbia panels in the Duomo at Florence, portray the history of music and dance from antiquity to the Empire. Two enormous tapestries depict the Creation and Fall, and Christ's Victory. An exotic touch is added by the magnificent Chinese vases and ginger jars, as well as a Japanese palanquin.

The fireplace in the dining room is carved with three biblical marriage scenes – Adam and Eve, Isaac and Rebecca, and Tobias and Sara – surmounted by musicians playing on a turreted balcony. In the library, the coats of arms on the ceiling beams celebrate marriages of the family, while those on the hood over the fireplace trace the Baron's own lineage.

It was 1900 before the floors were laid – to twelve different parquetry designs – and another fourteen before the last workman left the site. Although Cuypers fought hard to prevent his patron

Above: *The richly carved fireplace is a concealed minstrels' gallery, with a relief of the castle of love on the left.*

Left: *The* Ridderzaal, *or Knights' Hall. The chandelier is taken from Viollet-le-Duc's* Dictionary of Furniture.

Below: *In the dining room, the fireplace is carved with biblical scenes in a chivalric surround.*

from introducing alien elements, he respected him, writing in 1899: 'it always amazes me that there are so few people in the top class who have the gift of discernment and feel for fine colour and noble forms. Van Zuylen [the Baron] is in this respect still one of the best and he enjoys talking to me about it.' Upstairs, however, Cuypers lost control and the Baron turned to England. In March 1900, a Mr Shearburn of Maple's came to stay to measure bedrooms. These were furnished in fashionable Sheraton, Renaissance and Louis XIV styles. Ten English workmen who came over stayed in the *châtelet* rather than the village, 'in view of the anti-English feelings of the Dutch'.

Chivalrous display was accompanied by the latest technology. Many of the fireplaces contained not grates but large radiators. There was electricity from the start, with the bulbs carefully integrated into the architecture. De Haar had an impressive thirty bathrooms, of which all but five were en suite. The Baron insisted that the fittings in each should be different. 'De Haar should be like a private house, not a hotel,' he wrote.

The Baron was an early champion of both the motor car and the aeroplane, and a very large garage and stables were built near the house. With its park, formal gardens, *châtelet*, church and village, De Haar forms its own enclosed and secluded world. It remains a family home, run in a style that even the Baron's Rothschild wife would acknowledge as being correct. The whole village of Haarzuylens was moved several miles away to create greater privacy. Land was also acquired from neighbouring farmers. All this opened the way to lay out extensive formal gardens and a large park planted with 7,000 trees and a stable block next to the entrance gatehouse. Across the moat from the castle the so-called *châtelet* was built for informal use by the family. This was connected to the main building by a bridge and incorporated numerous features and materials salvaged from the nearby houses and farms that had been demolished.

In 1998 a select auction of a hundred works of art from De Haar was held by Christie's. This was prompted by problems discovered in the castle foundations below the moat. 'Within eight years, the edifice would crack and commence to crumble and return to the state of ruin in which my grandfather found it,' wrote Baron van Zuylen in a preface to the sale catalogue.

As the castle is open to the public for eleven months a year, receiving 60,000 visitors a year, the family were hoping for a state grant at the standard 70 per cent rate. The sums involved were vast, and the Department of Culture hesitated, but the sale precipitated a positive decision and repairs are now under way – further assisted by the proceeds of the auction. Hopefully this one sacrifice will have precluded the need for others.

Right: *In the library, the heraldry on the fireplace hood traces the Baron's lineage.*

TWENTY-FIVE

SKOKLOSTER

SWEDEN

In winter, the great lake in front of Skokloster freezes solid for many weeks, and curators and staff living on the far shore can drive to work across the ice, cutting their journey by three-quarters of an hour. In just such conditions a century and a half ago, the Frenchman Xavier Marmier set off on a cold morning with a guide who did not know his way. Soon he found himself lost in the middle of Lake Mälaren, forced to dismount from his exhausted and frost-covered horse while his companion tried in vain to remember the instructions he had been given in Uppsala. Suddenly, Marmier caught a glimpse of the castle and the great iron globes on top of the corner towers, visible above the snow-covered roofs. An hour later, he was sitting in a vaulted saloon in a large leather armchair, feeling like a Scottish laird, and blessing his absent host as a plate of venison and a bottle of Madeira were placed before him.

Skokloster retains the magic to this day. Although the house has been lived in for only quite short periods, and the family sold it to the state as a museum in 1967, the feeling it still conveys is that the fires only need to be lit, the beds made up and wine brought from the cellar, and one could then stay not merely in comfort but in full Baroque splendour.

Skokloster's rich contents remain in superb condition. Leather hangings are still brilliant in colour, magnificent tapestries have not faded in three centuries, and satins, silks, flock wallpapers and dornix (the poor man's tapestry) survive in abundance. Painted doors and dados remain fresh, and richly marbled chimneypieces stand in all the main rooms, while floors are the original sanded pine or polished limestone. Family portraits crowd the walls and regular inventories survive to tell where virtually every piece of furniture has stood for three hundred years.

The survival of Skokloster's interiors in such good condition is due, paradoxically, not to technology but the absence of it. Everything is the exact opposite of the requirements set down in museum conservation manuals. In winter, the temperature in the library may be 15 degrees Centigrade below zero, with relative humidity of 60 to 80 per cent, yet books are in perfect condition.

The grandeur of Skokloster is a reflection of Swedish power at its greatest extent in the seventeenth century. In the Middle Ages, the parish of Sko had belonged to a Cistercian nunnery. This had been confiscated by the Crown at the Reformation, though the nuns had been allowed to stay on until the end of the sixteenth century. In 1611, the King granted the estate to a young Estonian noble-man, Herman Wrangel – part of a policy intended to establish closer ties with the nobility in the Baltic territories. His son, Carl Gustav, born at Skokloster in 1613, was to become one of Sweden's greatest commanders, to be compared with Wallenstein in the Empire or Turenne in France.

The young Wrangel received much of his education travelling in Europe, enrolling at the University of Leyden in 1630. After a stay in Paris, he had joined the Swedish Army in Germany, rising to the rank of field marshal at the age of thirty-two. Success bred success: in 1657, he became Lord High Admiral and, seven years later, Marshal of the Realm.

The Italian diplomat Lorenzo Magalotti provides a vivid description: 'The Marshal of the Realm is tall and has an attractive though proud appearance; he is around sixty years of age or rather more ... He is well mannered, fond of display, munificent, a man of his word but quick-tempered and very susceptible to women. He has a great many interests, enjoys books and scientists ... He uses

Preceding pages (left): The first-floor corridor. The woodwork is original, but the paintwork, in tones of grey, dates from around 1750.
(right): Skokloster seen from the lake. The castle was built for the great Swedish commander Carl Gustav Wrangel in 1654–68.

Right: The King's Hall. The central panel of the ceiling portrays a warrior slaying a dragon, boldly breaking the pictorial bounds of the frame like the other motifs around it.

Above: The ante-chamber to the Countess's apartment, with gilt leather hangings and a marbled fireplace. The chandelier is of crystal.

Left: The dining room in the Brahe apartment, hung with 'Spanish' leather which has retained its original colour and lustre. The wooden chimneypiece was carved by the Stockholm mason Marcus Hebel.

money for buildings … He keeps a large household, has a big stable and displays great courtesy to those who visit him. With all this his residence has the appearance of belonging not to a distinguished gentleman but rather to a German prince.'

Carl Gustav had a strong interest in architecture, giving detailed instructions to his architects and builders and often changing the plans himself. There is a tradition, well established in the nineteenth century, that Skokloster is modelled on the great castle at Aschaffenburg on the River Main, which Wrangel and Turenne captured in 1646. The foundations of the eastern range overlooking the lake were laid in 1654, and the roof was finished three years later. By 1660, both eastern towers were complete. The western range, begun in 1661, was roofed in 1668 but left incomplete internally at Wrangel's death in 1676.

It was long thought that the architect of Skokloster was the King's architect, Jean de la Vallée, or Nicodemus the Elder. More recent research shows that the man principally responsible for the design was Caspar Vogel of Erfurt, northern Germany, who had helped reconstruct Wrangelsburg in Pomerania. Vogel's conservative bent helps to explain the slightly old-fashioned appearance of Skokloster; some modifications, presumably to add style, were made by the great Nicholas Tessin, who introduced the rustication.

Wrangel had married Anna Margereta von Haugwitz of Kable, near Magdeburg in Saxony, in 1640. She bore him eleven children, but all seven sons died before they came of age. Three daughters survived, and it was they, along with the daughter of a fourth, who inherited their father's vast estates. Skokloster went to the eldest, Margareta Juliana, the wife of Nils Brahe, whose family collections later greatly enriched the house. In 1701, she had the castle entailed, ensuring the survival of the house largely intact.

The Brahes had estates of their own and used Skokloster only as an occasional summer retreat. Throughout the eighteenth century, visitors were regularly shown around; in 1793, the armourer

provided 213 nights' lodging there, and for three weeks in summer
every room in the castle was full. Early in the twentieth century,
Skokloster passed to the von Essen fanily, and the arrangement of
rooms made in the 1930s by the Baroness von Essen largely
survives unchanged.

The twin apartments of Wrangel and his wife are on the first
floor, opening off a central saloon and forming a continuous
enfilade. The saloon is today known as the King's Hall, from the
portraits of Swedish kings that line the walls. Here is the first of a
series of splendid double-decker chimneypieces richly carved by
Marcus Hebel, this one in 1658. Built for show, these were
evidently inadequate to warm the rooms, as beside them,
throughout the house, large stoves were added within a few years.
One, clad in porcelain tiles, was supplied by Hindrich Thim of
Stockholm. Doors, window reveals and the low dado are painted
with specimen flowers. Most powerful of all are the boldly
modelled ceiling reliefs, all bursting out of their frames.

The Countess's ante-chamber has a ceiling with delicate stucco
reliefs by Johan Anthoni, dating from 1664. The chimneypiece is
painted in imitation of richly veined, deep-red marble and carries
figures of Fidelity and Fecundity. The leather hangings are
particularly rich, with silver and peppermint green predominating.
These were certainly imported from Amsterdam (the technique
passed from Spain to the Spanish Netherlands). In the Countess's
bedroom, Wrangel's initials are combined in the ceiling in a
virtuoso calligraphic display surrounded by a scatter of flowers –
the work of the Swede Nils Eriksson, dating from 1671.

In Wrangel's bedchamber, the curtains are usually kept drawn to
protect the patterned satin hangings of the state bed, which are

Above: *In the Count's bedchamber, the satin bed hangings
are embroidered with sequins, while to the left of the
fireplace, original striped woollen dornix hangings survive.*

Right: *The Countess's bedchamber. The tapestries, made in
Gouda in 1634–37 and signed T. Schaep, were probably
war booty seized by Wrangel in a raid over the ice on
Danish islands.*

inlaid with sequins and retain their pompoms and tassels. As the room with the highest dignity, the bedchamber has an elaborate ceiling of five circular panels emblazoned with arms and armour and Wrangel's initials spelt out in the centre with swords and muskets.

A very sympathetic and subtle restoration of the house was carried out in the early nineteenth century by Magnus Brahe, the secretary and confidante of Napoleon's Marshal Bernadotte, who took the Swedish throne as Karl XIV Johan. The King could not speak Swedish, so Brahe had the task of translating documents as well as effective control of access to the King. Brahe created a memorial room to Bernadotte in the tower room beyond Wrangel's bedchamber, with a larger-than-life-size statue of the King portrayed as Mars by the Swedish sculptor Niklas Byström.

Today, Skokloster is one of the very best-preserved houses in all of Europe, and credit for this is due in considerable part to the architect who has looked after it for many years, Ove Hidemark. The rich collections even include the tools Wrangel used for making models of buildings and fortifications, as well as one of his lathes.

Top: *The Bernadotte Room, created in the 1830s by Magnus Brahe as a memorial to the French marshal who became King Karl XIV Johan of Sweden.*

Above: *A row of seventeenth-, eighteenth- and nineteenth-century box-type close stools complete with padded seats.*

Left: *Looking along the lakefront. Skokloster's white walls and dark roofs stand out clearly for miles around.*

INDEX